SERIES TEACHING FILM AND MEDIA STUDIES

Teaching Digital Video Production

D0024804

Pete Fraser and Barney Oram

Series Editor: Vivienne Clark
Commissioning Editor: Wendy Earle

 Education

British Library Cataloguing-in-Publication Data
A catalogue record for this book is available in the British Library

ISBN 085170977X

First published in 2003 by the British Film Institute
21 Stephen Street, London W1T 1LN

Copyright © British Film Institute 2003
The copyright of this teaching guide belongs to the British Film Institute.

Student worksheets to support this guide are supplied at: www.bfi.org.uk/tfms
User name: **digital**   Password: **te2701di**

Design: Amanda Hawkes
Cover photographs: Courtesy of bfi Stills
Printed in Great Britain by Cromwell Press

www.bfi.org.uk

The British Film Institute gives everyone the opportunity to increase their understanding and
appreciation of film and television from around the world.

Contents

Introduction to the series   2

1 Introduction   3
Assessment contexts   3
A rationale for practical work   4
The place of the practical in AS and A2 specifications   6
How to use this guide   10
Schemes of work   11
    Scheme of work 1: Apple iMovie induction   12
    Scheme of work 2: Storyboard Production   14
    Scheme of work 3: Adobe Premiere induction   16
    Scheme of work 4: Making a music video   18

2 Equipment and principles   20
Industry background   20
Digital video in the classroom   21
Equipment and software   22
    Shooting   23
    Health and safety, loan and insurance   25
    Editing   27
    Editing software   29
A note on technical support   35
Organising and storing work   37

3 Hands on   38
Digital video induction routes   38
    Route 1: Apple iMovie   38
    Route 2: Adobe Premiere   47
Basic principles   50
Managing students: the role of the teacher   61
Evaluation and assessment   64

Managing bigger projects: Making a music video   66
A final word on creativity   73
Conclusion   73

Glossary   74

References and bibliography   77

Websites   79

Acknowledgements   82

Introduction to the series

The recent rapid growth of both Film and Media Studies post-16 has inevitably led to a demand for more teachers of these popular courses. But, given the comparatively recent appearance of both subjects at degree level (and limited availability of relevant post-graduate teaching courses), many new and experienced teachers from other disciplines are faced with teaching either subject for the first time, without a degree-level background.

In addition, the new post-16 specifications saw the arrival of new set topics and areas of study, and some of the specifications have changing topics, so there is a pressing need for up-to-date resources to help teacher preparation.

This series has been developed with these factors – and the busy teacher – in mind. Each title aims to provide teachers with an accessible reference resource, with essential topic content, as well as clear guidance on good classroom practice to improve the quality of their teaching and learning. Every author in the series is an experienced practitioner of Film and/or Media Studies at this level and many have examining/moderating experience.

Key features:

- Assessment contexts
- Suggested schemes of work
- Historical contexts (where appropriate)
- Key facts, statistics and terms
- Detailed reference to the key concepts of Film and Media Studies
- Detailed case studies
- Glossaries
- Bibliographies
- Student worksheets, activities and resources (available online) – ready to print and photocopy for the classroom.

Other titles in the series include:
Teaching Scriptwriting, Screenplays and Storyboards for Film and TV Production; Teaching TV Sitcom; Teaching TV News; Teaching Analysis of Film Language and Production; Teaching TV Soap Opera; Teaching Women and Film; Teaching Video Games; Teaching World Cinema; Teaching British Broadcasting since 1990; Teaching British Cinema since 1990; Teaching Film Censorship and Controversy; Teaching Television Language.

SERIES EDITOR: Vivienne Clark is a former Head of Film and Media Studies. She is an Advanced Skills Teacher; Associate Tutor of the British Film Institute; and Principal Examiner for A level Media Studies for one of the English awarding bodies. She is a freelance teacher trainer and writer on Media and Film Studies, with several published textbooks and teaching resources. She is also a course tutor on the *bfi*/Middlesex University MA level module: An Introduction to Media Education (distance learning).

Authors:
Pete Fraser is Chief Examiner of A level Media Studies for one of the English awarding bodies and Head of Media Studies at Long Road Sixth Form College, Cambridge, where he oversees one of the largest cohorts for the subject in the country. He has taught Media Studies for nearly 20 years, with a particular focus upon video work for the past decade. He regularly delivers INSET for teachers on both course management and practical work, particularly using Apple's iMovie.
Barney Oram also teaches Media Studies at Long Road and is an Assistant Examiner of A level Media Studies for one of the English awarding bodies. He is currently assisting an Institute of Education (London) research project on online gaming among teenagers, and working on a book about Audiences and Institutions for Philip Allan Updates.

Introduction

Assessment contexts

	Awarding body & level	Subject	Unit code	Module/Topic
✓	WJEC AS Level	Film Studies	FS1	Making Meaning 1: Practical Approaches to Learning – Creative Work – film screenplays/storyboards
✓	WJEC A2 Level	Film Studies	FS4	Making Meaning 2: Practical Approaches to Learning – Creative Work – screenplays, storyboards and short filmmaking
✓	OCR AS Level	Media Studies	2730	Foundation Production – video/film/TV and pre-production
✓	OCR A2 Level	Media Studies	2733	Advanced Production – video/film/TV and pre-production
✓	AQA AS Level	Media Studies	MED2	Practical Production – video/film/TV and pre-production
✓	WJEC AS Level	Media Studies	ME3	Making Media Texts – video/film/TV and pre-production
✓	SQA Higher	Media Studies	D334 12	Media Production – video
✓	SQA Advanced Higher	Media Studies	D334 13	Media Production – video

This pack is also relevant to the teaching of practical media production assessments (film/TV/video) in the following specifications, as well as for Lifelong Learning and international courses:

- OCR – GNVQ and AVCE
- Ed-Excel – GNVQ and AVCE
- BTech National Diploma

Please note that when an assessment context is being discussed here, the authors use the terms 'candidate' for 'student' and 'Centre' for school or college.

A rationale for practical work

'Because of the dumbing down of the youth and the erosion of their standards, we now insist that students create and use pinhole cameras for their production work, which we find to be just as creatively appropriate as all this new-fangled Macintosh business.' *(Julian McDougall, August 2002, email posted on OCR Media Studies site)*

This tongue-in-cheek contribution to the OCR Media teachers' emailing list comes at a time when many schools and colleges are investing in digital technology to enable their students to produce better work and to give them a much greater insight into the process of meaning-making through editing. The bewildering choice of cameras, edit programs and even computers can leave teachers wishing that they'd stuck to using scissors, card, pencils and the storyboard.

However, writing as teachers at a very large sixth form college, which has invested heavily in hardware over the past three years, we can vouch for the venture being worthwhile. This book is designed to help advise on the basics, so that many more students will gain access to the technology and the opportunities for both learning and creativity which come with it and so that many more teachers will feel confident about taking the plunge.

● Why do practical work in Media Studies?

A few years ago this question was a prominent one. The polarisation between the old Film Studies GCE O level with its entirely theoretical model of assessment and the CSE in Television Studies was followed by a gap between A level and GCSE Media Studies, both arguably 'theory-led' and vocational courses like the NVQ. David Buckingham identified four 'versions' of practical production in 1995, which informed these courses:

- Practical work as self-expression (from a progressive Art and English tradition);
- Practical work as a method of learning in itself (promoting group work, social and communication skills);
- Practical work as vocational training (or rather as pre-vocational training in FE colleges);
- Practical work as deconstruction (experimenting with the codes of the media in order to challenge their dominance).

Elements of all these approaches fed into the GCSE and A level courses introduced in the mid- to late 1980s and while influential voices in media education such as Bob Ferguson and Len Masterman questioned the value of practical work, those opting for courses often saw it as a key motivating factor.

All four 'versions' still co-exist, but the major change of the last decade has been the introduction of new digital technologies, which enable the construction of media products by Media students to take place in ways that were previously unimaginable, alongside a massive expansion in the subject area, which has pushed it closer to the mainstream of the curriculum.

So what is the rationale behind practical work in post-16 media education? The four versions each have their part to play, but the transformation wrought by digital perhaps suggests a fifth – to enable young people to become active participants in whatever kind of 'digital democracy' might exist in the 21st century. This goes beyond the old traditional print literacies and into the possibilities opened up by new media, such as the internet, and for means of expression across verbal and visual forms.

● Practical work as self-expression

We shall return to notions of 'creativity' later, but would argue that an element of 'self-expression' should be present in media practical work, while cautioning against its more romantic manifestations. However, we think that teacher-directed projects, rather than 'free choice' for students, are more likely to lead to successful outcomes.

● Practical work as a method of learning in itself

Practical work as a method of learning in itself is also crucial; there are still relatively few spaces in the curriculum where collaborative work by students can be credited. Issues are raised about the management and assessment of group work to which we will return later.

● Practical work as vocational training

With the line now blurred between domestic- and industry-standard edit and image programs, it is possible to argue that practical work has more of an element of vocational training than previously and that many students will emerge from 16–19 education with a significant level of expertise on equipment which will be useful to them in the job market. Many students discover talents and aptitudes that they were previously unaware of and this, in turn, creates expectations of what they wish to study at degree level or to choose as a career.

● Practical work as deconstruction

One of the problems with the 'Practical work as deconstruction' approach, in early 1990s media practical work, seemed to be a privileging of 'alternative' and *avant-garde* approaches which often meant students were only credited for rule-breaking and not for knowing the rules in the first place. It could be argued that students can only truly challenge the rules once they know them properly – hence the approach of this pack is to train students to use camera and editing properly before they try to break conventions. Nonetheless the very act of constructing a media text which 'makes sense' involves learning about how to deconstruct existing texts.

If a rationale is needed to convince others, it is worth emphasising that Media Studies can play an important role in the acquisition of advanced ICT skills. Ultimately institutions should need little convincing of the usefulness of Media courses in an age when student numbers generate income. However they usually need to be convinced of the value of spending money on equipment to run such courses.

The place of the practical in AS and A2 specifications

In this section we shall briefly outline the practical components of WJEC Film Studies and each of the three Media specifications (AQA, OCR and WJEC). For more detail and up-to-date versions of the respective requirements, readers are advised to visit the relevant websites and view the awarding bodies' specifications. All courses tie their practical element to written evaluations and break down the marking so that a range of skills are assessed. All Media specifications offer assessed practical at AS but only OCR has a further assessed practical at A2. In each case, there is no compulsion for moving image work, as there are print and audio (and sometimes ICT) options but some of the most exciting and productive work undoubtedly takes place in the form of video.

● Film Studies A2

While AS Film Studies offers a screenwriting or storyboarding option (worth 16% of AS), the only technologically-based unit in the course is at A2, where filmmaking is one of the three options on offer (20% of A2, 10% of A level).

The options are: film journalism, screenwriting, film/video-making. Each project must include writing on aims and rationale (500 words) and self-evaluation (500 words), worth 20 marks in total. Thirty marks are allocated to the product: the candidate should demonstrate an understanding and appreciation of the forms and conventions of the medium chosen, and attempt to work creatively with the tensions between competing meaning structures such as genre and *auteur*.

The project involves the production of either an extract from a film or a complete short film of three to five minutes in length. This may be produced individually or in a group of up to three students – each of whose contribution must be clearly identifiable for assessment purposes. Credit is given for creative and organisational skills within the group.

There are advantages and disadvantages to such a project: the open subject matter can be seen as liberating for students' creativity but it can also result in long periods of agonising over what to do and how to get started. The stipulation, that the project must be rooted in working creatively with tensions between competing meaning structures, is a rather subtle one for students of this age group to grasp and can lead to projects which are too vague or pretentious. In the end, it might be sensible for teachers to put their own limitations on such a project within the broader parameters set by the board to encourage more focused planning by students.

● AQA Media Studies AS

In this course, the coursework component for A2 comprises a research project which means that the only opportunity for assessed practical work is at AS. The work here, like that for Film Studies, has to be loosely rooted in the work done for theoretical units. The unit is worth 40% of AS (20% of full A level).

The practical production is designed to show that candidates have acquired the appropriate skills to enable them to use the chosen technologies competently. It will also demonstrate their knowledge and application of relevant Key Concepts, both in their analysis of their chosen topic (the Brief) and the practical production itself.

The final assessment requirement includes the writing of an initial brief of 750 words (worth 10%), a finished product which demonstrates a candidate's skill in using one or more appropriate media technologies, arising directly from the candidate's study of one of the four topics in AS Module 2 (*Film and Broadcast Fiction, British Newspapers, Documentary, Advertising and Marketing*) and finally an evaluation of approximately 1000 words which critiques the work and shows how it is linked to the particular aspects of Module 2 which it has explored.

Again there are pros and cons to this assignment. The brief is open but there is a clear requirement to link it to material explored in another AS module, which does help narrow it a bit. The requirement for students to create their own brief again needs teacher assistance if they are to remain focused. The assessment criteria are very generalised, which may be seen as a strength or a weakness depending upon your perspective. Clearly there are several different options for moving image work.

● WJEC Media

Again the A2 coursework is research-based, leaving the only assessed practical at AS. In this case the production of exercises is the focus, rather than a big project. As with AQA, the project is worth 40% of AS, 20% of the full A level.

This unit is designed to enable candidates to demonstrate their knowledge and understanding of media practice through their engagement with the planning, processing and evaluation stages of media productions. The aim is to focus on three small tasks, which will enable them to develop a range of pre-production skills, production skills and key skills. Candidates are required to produce technically competent pieces given the media technology available to them.

The unit should be teacher-directed and although candidates will be required to undertake work for their portfolios individually, it is envisaged that Centres will introduce and set tasks on a whole class basis. It is expected that candidates will have been taught to use the equipment available to them prior to undertaking their production piece.

Candidates will be required to submit a portfolio of three pieces of work. Two pieces will demonstrate pre-production planning techniques and one piece will focus on production. The pieces must be from two different media forms. Within these short pieces candidates will be required to demonstrate their understanding of the key media concepts of genre, narrative and audience together with their ability to evaluate media production work.

Though the emphasis on practical work throughout the course is clearly high, with three pieces to be produced, there are limitations here – notably the requirement for individual work, the need to work in two different media and particularly the fact that only pre-production is assessed in two of the tasks. It can also seem a considerable investment of student time and effort for a relatively small proportion of the marks. Again there is clearly potential for digital video (DV) work.

● OCR Media

OCR is the only course to allow an assessed practical in both years of the A level, each worth 40% of that year's assessment. At AS there is less freedom than in the other specifications, although the practical work does not have to relate to the content of any other unit. Instead there are six set briefs, each with a specified target audience, to be undertaken either as individual or group work (maximum group number is four candidates). The production itself is to be accompanied by an individual production log undertaken by each candidate (2000 words).

There are options in print, radio and web design in addition to two moving image tasks (from September 2003, either the opening sequence of a new children's TV programme or the opening sequence of a film thriller). The unit is marked for planning (30 marks), construction (60 marks) and writing (30 marks).

In addition, the OCR specification demands particular technical competences for assessment in each medium so that for moving image work the following are all assessed:

- holding a shot steady;
- framing a shot;
- using a variety of shot distances;
- shooting material appropriate to the task set;
- editing so that meaning is apparent to the viewer;
- using varied shot transitions, captions and other effects selectively and where appropriate for the task set;
- using sound with images.

At A2 the brief is open but students are expected to work in a different medium from AS (though for this purpose film, TV and video count as three different media). The pattern of assessment is broadly similar to AS, although the writing needs to be 3000 words in length, and the expectation for construction is that A2 work will demonstrate a higher standard of technical skills than AS.

Again there are advantages and disadvantages to this model. Centres wanting a lot of assessed practical work obviously get more of it with OCR than with any of the other specifications; at the same time, more is expected, both in terms of the assessment criteria for construction of finished products and in the writing (which is much longer). At AS, choice is quite restricted with the set briefs, though for assessment purposes this may have its advantages. They are also deliberately chosen so that they do not overlap with any content of the other AS units, which makes them different from all other specifications where practical projects arise from units of theoretical/analytical study. At A2, the free choice may be too much for students to handle and as with Film Studies, teachers may prefer to set the task, so the choice just becomes free from being set by the board rather than complete freedom for students.

Clearly there are areas of overlap between the specifications in terms of assessment objectives, but whichever one you choose, these objectives need to be read carefully to see how far the practical production is theory-led or skills-based.

● Typical video projects

As we have seen, there are quite specific criteria for choosing the task in each specification, even within moving image work. For Film Studies, the main criteria are time (3–5 minutes duration) and the 'tension between competing meaning structures', while for OCR Media, the set briefs define quite strictly what can be produced in generic terms. The AQA and WJEC Media lie somewhere in between.

The defining feature of all such productions is that they should be small and manageable by both students and Centres. There is no point in letting students embark on a project which will take months to finish or is going to run to even six or seven minutes in length. Such projects only succeed in very rare instances with exceptional students. One of the reasons is that the longer and more complex the project, the more can go wrong. If students are to show off what they can do rather than demonstrate all the mistakes that they are capable of making, then shorter projects are clearly to their advantage.

Typical projects in non-fiction include pieces from news broadcasts and extracts from documentaries, though we have also seen entertaining and well-constructed instructional fitness and sports videos. Adverts, TV title sequences and film trailers are common projects, similar to the opening sequences of films. The most common video task at A2 for OCR is undoubtedly the music video.

How to use this guide

This guide is intended to provide a clear and accessible introduction to digital video production. The aim is to help you to enable your students to create finished products to as professional a standard as possible within a set time limit. It is based on our experience in developing digital video production courses at our college, and will hopefully provide you with a useful starting point for developing your own courses.

The scope of this guide cannot include a detailed user guide to the various software programs mentioned. For this you will need to refer to the user manuals and other guidebooks relating to the software programs you use.

It is important that the teacher of Film or Media Studies post-16 is thoroughly familiar with the theory and practice of filmmaking. There are opportunities for overlap between units of the various specifications, for example, between video production and textual analysis of the technical aspects of moving image extracts and of film narrative, which can be beneficially exploited in course design, in order to reinforce students' learning.

This guide necessarily deals mostly with the practicalities of digital video production, but at the end of this book are suggestions for books and teaching packs, which support the teaching and learning of filmmaking theory and narrative construction, etc and can be used in conjunction with this practical guide. In particular two titles in this series will be useful to developing a good digital video production course:

- *Teaching Scriptwriting, Screenplays and Storyboards for Film and TV Production,* Mark Readman;
- *Teaching Analysis of Film Language and Production*, Elaine Scarratt.

Around the country there are pockets of considerable teacher expertise in a wide variety of programs and processes. This is largely due to the enthusiasm and commitment of individuals who have funded their own resources and learning over the years, rather than to any systematic programme of continuing professional development. But senior managers of schools or colleges and national professional policy should not depend on this. Adequate time for teachers' professional development should be factored into the funding and running of Film or Media courses, so that teachers can become familiar with these programs before using them with students.

The **schemes of work** outlined below offer four different approaches to digital video production in schools.

The following chapters provide the information and background you need to develop a scheme of work to suit the needs of your students.

- **Chapter 2 – Equipment and principles**: provides background on the development of digital video equipment and advice on buying cameras and accessories, and computers and software for editing.
- **Chapter 3 – Hands on**: provides detailed guidelines to running a digital video induction programme, evaluation and assessment processes and producing a music video.
- At the end of the book there is a bibliography and a list of website addresses of suppliers and other useful contacts to help set up your course.

The worksheets to support these activities are available at www.bfi.org.uk/tfms. To access the pages, when asked, enter username: **digital** and the password: **te2701di**. If you have any problems, email: education.resources@bfi.org.uk.

Schemes of work

It is essential that you become familiar with the featured software programs before embarking on these schemes of work. There are many simplified manuals for programs such as Adobe Photoshop, Adobe Première and Apple iMovie, such as the *For Dummies* and *For Idiots* series and classroom guides published by the software manufacturers, which can be sourced from an online book supplier, such as Amazon. Most programs come with official manuals (although these are not always accessible) and tutorials. The scope of this teaching pack cannot hope to cover the technical detail of the software programs themselves; it focuses on how to teach digital video editing.

NB In these schemes of work each lesson lasts one hour, ten minutes.

● Scheme of work 1: Apple iMovie induction

This nine-session unit has been designed as an introduction to the equipment, and how to use it and the software. It then offers preparation for practical projects, including some work on how editing operates in the process of telling stories and how different types of shot might contribute to meaning in film and television.

Aims:
- To achieve basic knowledge of the computers including effective filing;
- To introduce the main features of Adobe Photoshop;
- To introduce editing techniques;
- To introduce the main features of Apple iMovie;
- To introduce how to use the camera.

Outcomes:
- Adobe Photoshop productions including a club flyer;
- Completed Apple iMovie tutorial;
- Completed 'Horror stills' exercise;
- Completed 'Phone call' exercise;
- Analysis of finished products: especially strengths and weaknesses;
- 'Digital driving test' for equipment and programs.

Session 1   Introduction to iMac and filing system

Demonstration of Photoshop via digital projector

In pairs, students create a canvas and import digital photo of themselves, add text and try out some effects to create a self-portrait, 'Me'

Finished canvas 'Me' project may be printed out for display

Session 2   Demonstration of more Photoshop techniques

In pairs, students create canvas and import images from the image bank to create 'Club flyer' using a range of further effects; finished project may be printed out for display

Session 3   *Picture Power* exercise, 'Pursued' in pairs – understanding editing's contribution to storytelling

Worksheet 1

Finished work demonstrated by pairs circulating room to observe others' projects

Session 4   iMovie tutorial – understanding the basics of the program

In pairs, students have to reconstruct the sequence cutting it down to 30 seconds using three effects, three transitions and three sound effects

Finished sequences viewed by all circulating the room

Worksheet 2

Session 5   Horror stills 1

Teacher demonstration of camera and explanation of how to set up tripod plus all basic rules of camera use

Groups each show that they can set up camera and tripod

Groups are given 30 minutes on the premises to shoot stills from an imaginary horror film using only resources and locations immediately to hand

When they return they download footage into iMovie file

Worksheet 3 – Session 1

Session 6   Horror Stills 2

Teacher demonstration of how to re-touch an image in Photoshop and then import it into iMovie (cut off limbs and paint blood!)

Using music pre-loaded into files, groups of four construct a sequence based on their images including at least one image re-touched in Photoshop.

Finished sequences exported to tape and viewed in subsequent lesson in parallel 'theory' classroom sessions

Worksheet 3 – Session 2

Session 7   Phone call 1

Groups given instructions to shoot moving images with use of clapperboard

Shot-by-shot rules explained and limitations of sound on the camera

Groups of four go out to shoot

Worksheet 4 – Session 1

Session 8   Phone call 2

Groups edit their footage according to the rules given

Finished work exported to video and used in parallel classroom session

Worksheet 4 – Session 2

Session 9   Digital driving test

Observed by a member of staff individually, each student has to go through a series of 20 tasks to prove they can use camera, tripod, computer and iMovie

Any task they fail, is immediately demonstrated again

Worksheet 5

● Scheme of work 2: Storyboard production

(Based on activities developed by Mark Readman for *Teaching Scriptwriting, Screenplays and Storyboards in Film and TV Production.*)
This six-week block is designed to develop visual awareness and the specific skills connected with storyboard production. It incorporates some prescriptive sketching and sequencing exercises, as well as some consideration of story and genre, and results in a final original product.

Aims:
- To understand terminology relating to shot type and movement;
- To understand the generation of meaning through *mise en scène;*
- To understand the generation of meaning through sequencing;
- To acquire and practise skills in storyboard artistry.

Outcomes:
- Close analysis of shot types and sequences;
- Production of controlled storyboard sequences;
- Production of a storyboard extract.

Week 1   Introduction to basic shot types and simple sketching techniques

Introduction to glossary of key technical terms and demonstration of representing movement in storyboards

Representation of movement within shot and of camera

Construction of a ten-shot storyboard sequence from a given list of prescribed shots

Camera terms student notes

Week 2 *Mise en scène* analysis of moving image sequences (eg opening of *Taxi Driver*, 'stalking scene' from *Tightrope*) to illustrate significance of position, movement, lighting and framing

Sketching exercise – replicating key shots from examples analysed

Group exercise – construction of a 20-shot storyboard sequence from a list of prescribed shots

Storyboard   /   Shot list

Week 3 Presentation of storyboard sequences (possibly on OHTs) and discussion of successful and less successful aspects. Comparison with *Buffy* extract (especially if storyboard is realised on video)

Examination of 'cross cut' sequence from appropriate film or TV programme and discussion of tempo and framing

Small group exercise – storyboard 10–15 shot sequence cutting between two locations and creating suspense

Storyboard   /   Shot list

Week 4 Presentation of sequences and discussion focusing on duration, framing and sequencing

Examination of existing storyboard example (eg *Alien*, *Mission to Mars*) – identification of techniques, conventions and effects previously discussed

Genre recognition based on single frames – key visual conventions

Small group exercise – produce single frames which evoke generic associations (eg horror, Western, film noir)

Week 5 Brief introduction to Three Act Structure

Practical group exercise – based on a genre and a protagonist, develop story outline to include description of key story events and resolution

Presentation and evaluation of story proposals

Week 6 Group exercise – Selection of key sequence from story outline and consideration of how to represent it visually

Pitch visual ideas for sequence – evaluate in the light of feedback

Produce storyboard extract

'Carousel' activity to get peer feedback on storyboard

● Scheme of work 3: Adobe Premiere Induction

This seven-session unit has been designed as an introduction to the main features of Adobe Premiere with particular reference to those needed for the task of constructing a music video; it is thus undertaken at the end of Year 12 after considerable work using iMovie.

Aims:
- To achieve understanding of the main features of Premiere;
- To ensure effective use of the program and of filing/settings to avoid any problems.

Outcomes:
- A series of completed exercises each demonstrating a grasp of a particular aspect of the program.

Session 1   Teacher demonstration using laptop and digital projector

Settings in Premiere

Starting a new project

Saving and filing

Importing clips – files and folders

Using the timeline

Audio synch

Moving clips

Students practise the various features they have been shown, working in pairs on the computers, then work on reconstructing a short film cut into clips and imported in a folder. Finally they match the clips to the soundtrack.

Session 2   Teacher demonstration using laptop and digital projector

Setting in and out points

Trimming clips

Fading clips

Previewing fades

Changing clip speed

Students in pairs work on editing some clips provided in folders, trying out features demonstrated

Session 3   Teacher demonstration

Using synch mode

Adding tracks, lip-synching

Students in pairs work on lip-synching material from a folder imported into the program

Session 4   Further work following up Session 3

Session 5   Teacher demonstration

Transitions

Adding effects

In pairs, students try out some transitions and effects on imported material

Session 6   Teacher demonstration

Importing Photoshop files

Transparency

Motion settings

Scratch effects

In pairs, students have to animate an image of a plane flying across a landscape

Session 7   Teacher demonstration

Titles

Using techniques learnt in all sessions, students in pairs animate some titles

● Scheme of work 4: Making a music video

This scheme of work offers some broad introduction to the music industry, with a particular focus on the music video, before students are set the coursework task. Thereafter all work is in groups planning, shooting and editing until the deadline. The final part of the project then concentrates upon the written evaluation.

Aims:
- To understand the main purposes of a music video;
- To obtain a methodology suitable for the analysis of any music video;
- To gain a suitable grasp of the techniques needed to make a good student video;
- To produce a good piece of practical work to the deadline;
- To produce a good written evaluation.

Outcomes:
- A music video for an unknown band and a 3000 word evaluation.

Session 1   Introduction to project dates and deadlines

Class brainstorm 'What is a music video?'

Teacher-led introduction to Goodwin's method of analysing music video

Application of Goodwin's criteria to an example

Session 2   Continue work from Session 1

Groups to discuss various aspects of Goodwin's method and apply it to example shown in class

Group feedback collected together to form overall analysis of video

Session 3   Teacher-chosen range of music videos

Class screenings and discussion of conventions and application of Goodwin's methods

Session 4   Examples of old student music videos screened by teacher

Class discussion of strengths and weaknesses

Session 5   Guest speakers: music video directors screen and discuss their work and answer questions from students

Session 6   'The pitch' – example of a pitch for a music video discussed in class and broken down as a model for students

Session 7	Outline of task on paper gone through by teacher
	Class split into groups and CDs of possible choices distributed (range of genres)
Session 8	Groups listen to CDs and make notes to narrow down choices
Session 9	Groups prepare pitch for their chosen act
Session 10	Each group pitches for chosen act in front of rest of class
	Teacher makes notes and decides which will be given their choices
Session 11	Choices announced, any re-pitching begins
Sessions 12–27	Planning, shooting, editing
Sessions 28–9	Screening, discussion and analysis of finished videos Feedback from audience
Sessions 30–4	Advice on writing, time for help with drafts of writing and more individual feedback

2

Equipment and principles

Industry background

Digital video (DV) and computer editing programs have not only changed the way films are made but also the people who are making them. There is an ever-growing number of good quality digital cameras on the market as well as powerful and easy to use editing software. This has the potential to alter filmmaking as we know it and allow a new generation to alter our expectations and challenge the traditional distribution channels. It is an exciting time to be involved in this area.

This section covers a range of issues about DV and its role in the film industry; it gives examples of films produced on DV and discusses issues surrounding them. It demonstrates how DV has major benefits for the independent and amateur filmmaker, including in the classroom context.

Between 1998 and 1999 Next Wave Films (an American company and part of the Independent Film Channel) saw the percentage of digital submissions rise to over 34% of all requests for finishing funds. In 2001 66% of the features added to their database were shot on DV. This illustrates the uptake among filmmakers with limited financial resources; no other development in cinema's history has lowered the cost of filmmaking as effectively as DV cameras and post-production software. This has resulted in the technology becoming available to a whole new market.

Industry take up of DV has been slow given that digital editing has long been established in the form of AVID (the industry standard system). There are a number of factors that have helped contribute to this, including the reluctance of studios to alter the distribution and exhibition process and the resistance of the majority of directors who still prefer to make films using celluloid. Films shot on DV still need to be transferred to film as (at the time of writing) only a handful of cinemas, both in Europe and the US, have digital projectors. A rare recent example was *Toy Story 2* (John Lasseter, 1999), which was the first digital film to be digitally projected, but only in one of the London Leicester Square cinemas.

However, only a handful of directors have shot films using DV, the majority of these being art-house or experimental films. For example, *Time Code* (Mike

Figgis, 1999) was funded by Sony as an experiment to see how DV cameras could be used; it is notable that the director is well known for art-house films rather than big budget efforts. *Time Code* experimented with the possibilities of DV cameras and editing by dividing the screen into four; this also meant that the film had a limited appeal. *Dancer in the Dark* (Lars Von Trier, 2000) cost $13million and used DV cameras, allowing the director to shoot more on a smaller budget. Independent filmmakers are the force behind the development of DV as a dominant format. These filmmakers are breaking new ground as far as Hollywood is concerned; the major studios are reluctant to commit to a new format that could radically alter the traditional distribution process.

Now that major directors are beginning to use DV cameras, the speed of change is likely to increase. Shooting *Traffic* (2000) with DV cameras allowed the director, Steven Soderbergh, to produce two films within a year, such is the speed that DV offers, as well as to use the distinctive colour filters that are a feature of the film. George Lucas shot the second *Star Wars* prequel, *Attack of the Clones* (2002) using DV cameras. His desire to use DV forced Sony and Panavision to produce a high spec camera and this is likely to improve take up among directors who claim that celluloid produces a better quality picture.

The internet will also have a major impact on the distribution process, allowing the low budget DV filmmaker an easily accessible distribution channel. As both the hardware and the software become cheaper it could open the floodgates for the next generation of filmmakers.

Digital Video in the classroom

Digital video has the potential to radically alter the way both teachers and students approach practical work. With DV, picture information is stored digitally. This means that it can be copied and edited without the loss of quality that you get when editing VHS tapes. Analogue video editing, using tapes, is *linear* – shots are placed one after another to construct a film sequentially from beginning to end; digital editing on computer is *non-linear* – students can do their editing in any order and revise their work easily. Furthermore, instead of being something that is produced behind closed doors without the involvement of the teacher, DV is so accessible and versatile that practical work can now form the centre of the course, informing theoretical work as well as developing a range of other skills such as teamwork, communication and visual awareness.

However, careful planning is paramount to a successful student experience; without close guidance and constructive feedback, DV can become a problem, while, with close management and clear guidelines, it is likely to be the most positive aspect of the course.

Ten years ago DV equipment was prohibitively expensive and still in a developmental stage. Now it is more accessible in terms of both cost and ease of use. Recent developments mean that hardware and software are now available to suit all budgets. This section covers a range of issues surrounding both hardware and software, including the choice of cameras, editing packages, and computer set-ups. It is a starting point and provides basic information that will be useful if you are considering investing in DV technology. You will need to do further research to become fully up-to-speed with all the issues involved, and further sources of information are provided at the back of this book.

It is essential that you are comfortable with the technology, and you need to learn about the software and hardware, and how to construct videos. The acquisition of such ICT and audiovisual skills should form a core part of Media or Film Studies teachers' initial training and continuing professional development. Gradually, more training courses and resources are becoming available. However, schools and colleges need to appreciate the time and money that is needed to support such professional development, especially given the high student recruitment and retention (not to mention added value, in terms of exam results) usually delivered by Film or Media courses.

Equipment and software

● Budget and ratios

In terms of an overall budget you can only get what your institution gives you, but often by asking for the earth, you might just get the moon! It is also important to anticipate that a one-off capital expense will not be sufficient and so allow for year-on-year additions, upgrades and replacements in any bids; you are not serving your students well by trying to do Media Studies 'on the cheap'. Tie your bids to ICT priorities, as well as making reference to the new post-16 funding requirements, and any other grants that might be on offer. It is difficult to be precise on camera:student ratios, but as a rule of thumb it is better to buy as much equipment as you can rather than just have one or two expensive 'special' set-ups. If students are to have a lot of access to cameras to improve the quality of their work, several cameras need to be available.

It is probably sensible to have two cameras as your starting point (with a bag and tripod and spare battery for each) for up to 20 students. Then work on the basis that every additional cohort of 20 students needs another camera added, so 40 students = 3 cameras, 60 = 4 and so on. At our own college we have 15 cameras between 600 students at the time of writing, which is not our ideal ratio, but we manage well enough.

● Shooting

Hardware

You will need
- Cameras
- Tripods
- Bags
- Extra batteries
- DV tapes
- Lights
- External microphones.

What should you look for in a camera?
The type of camera that you will buy will depend upon a range of factors including your budget and the number of students. DV cameras can cost anywhere between £500–£3500 in the non-professional range. The camera that you buy must be compatible with the hardware that you buy. The standardisation of DV means that all you need to import DV footage is a FireWire compliant capture card. This is also known as either an IEEE 1394 card (or i-Link if the camera is a Sony).

Here is a range of features you will need, and their functions.

- **DV-in port** – An essential feature if you want to record an edited production back out to DV tape, realistically the easiest way to maintain perfect picture quality.
- **DV-out port** – Needed to transfer the DV footage to the computer, the camera is connected to the computer via a FireWire (IEEE 1394). The camera you buy must be compatible with the FireWlre card you have. Macs come with FireWire ports as standard.
- **S-Video port** – Useful for a higher quality export than the normal RGB cables.
- **Manual focus** – A feature that allows the user greater control of the quality of the footage shot. Often auto focus will result in a slight blurring of shots, especially if there is movement in a sequence. This is because the lens will try to refocus on the moving object.
- **Size** – Many DV cameras are becoming smaller but this does not necessarily mean they are becoming better. Miniaturisation may result in parts being harder to use or more fragile; you should buy a camera that is fairly robust.
- **Battery life** – This can make a huge difference for student filmmakers; if possible you need to know how long the battery will last (45 minutes is about standard). For most makes of camera it is possible to buy longer lasting batteries, but this should be checked out before you buy a camera.

There are also features that should be avoided. These include:

- **Bottom-loading tapes** – These mean dismantling the camera from the tripod to load another tape, which can be time consuming.
- **Special formats** – Sony, for example, have recently released a new format specifically for its own cameras; this can present problems if a number of cameras are bought over time.

Overall the choice of camera is likely to be dictated by budget, resources and personal preferences. As they will be used by students, the cameras you buy should be robust and reliable. DV cameras for basic use are constantly coming down in price and by shopping around and getting educational prices wherever possible, it is feasible to get them for less than £500 each.

Tripod

Since DV cameras are much lighter than analogue cameras, tripods can now be more lightweight too. Provided it is used properly and students are given proper training in how to erect it, fit the camera and disassemble, you can use tripods in the £30 range. The clip, which attaches camera to tripod, is easily lost so buy some spares (less than £5 each). Jessops have a good range of low-budget tripods which are fine for the basic lighter cameras.

Bag

These rarely come with the camera so you need to buy them separately, but again expect to pay no more than £30. Check all dimensions before ordering. The bag just needs room for the basic accessories (leads, spare battery, mains adapter/charger). It is to transport the camera safely and to keep it dry, so it needs padding and to be watertight. Make sure the strap is fitted so that it is convenient for student use. A small laminated tag, fixed to the strap or bag, which shows a checklist of the bag's full contents, is a useful reminder to students and teachers when checking equipment out and in.

Extra battery

As noted above, the battery which comes with the camera may not last long enough and may take a bit of a hammering from frequent student use, which will reduce its working life. So it is worth investing in a long-life version as back-up and later as replacement. This will be expensive (a three-hour battery can be well over £100) but in the end is necessary unless you have a very small class.

DV tapes

Tapes are potentially the cheapest item on your list. If you order in bulk you can pay under £2 per tape (a quarter of the price you might be charged in a high street store).

Light

Many video cameras have a built-in light but these are not strong enough for most night shooting, so students should be advised not to rely upon them to illuminate a scene effectively and they will need to use additional lighting. Even a bedside lamp or desk-light create useful effects, but a builder's light is very effective and is a worthwhile investment at around £40 from DIY suppliers (custom-made stage lights are much more expensive).

External microphone

The integral microphone in a standard camcorder is not ideal for student video work involving dialogue. Internal microphones tend to pick up all extraneous sound, which often muffles the intended dialogue altogether. Students will need an external microphone, if you are contemplating projects which involve a lot of dialogue. Before buying a camera, check that it has inputs for an external microphone.

Omni-directional mics pick up all sound from a wide area; uni-directional mics record sound at a shorter distance (ideal for a reporter, for example); tie-mics allow for freedom of movement in an interview and are less conspicuous than hand-held ones.

Where to buy?

Not from your local electrical superstore. Try education departments of main dealers, such as Apple and Sony. Buy camcorder magazines and trawl through the display adverts; likewise computer magazines, as sometimes you can get camera equipment as part of a deal with computers. Compare prices and get at least three parallel quotes; you can often save as much as 20% (ie get 20% more equipment for your bid price) in a comparison of three quotations.

● Health and safety, loan and insurance

There are some basic rules about camera use which students need to be taught from the outset. Provided you have bought cameras which are easy to use, it should be possible to teach them the basics in a matter of minutes (on/off functions, record and pause, zoom function, viewfinder) but at the same time it is important to advise on safe use of the equipment.

Equipment safety: Cardinal rules

1 When the camera is not in use it should be carried in the bag, which should be properly secured via zip or straps.
2 When using the camera, the person doing the recording should **always** hang it around his/her neck using the long strap and should hold the camera with the hand strap.

3 If the tripod is being used, one person should be responsible for carrying it and setting it up, ensuring legs are of equal length and that all clips are in place. He/she then holds the tripod while the camera operator attaches the camera and no-one lets go until all are sure that everything is secure and safe.

4 Dismantling is done in the same way. The camera is NEVER to be carried on the tripod.

5 If it starts to rain, the camera is to be immediately replaced in the bag.

6 Tapes are never inserted or removed by students, but fitted in advance by staff, so there is no reason to open the mechanism.

7 You need to check equipment back in at the end of a shooting session. (Even after as little as 20 minutes of excitement, there is a tendency for camera bags to be left in the canteen.)

Student safety

You must be absolutely clear about where students can and cannot go and what they can and cannot do. There have been a number of scare stories involving Media students taking creativity too far (usually involving pretend guns and the police helicopter being scrambled) but even on the school or college premises, they do have a tendency to annoy staff and get themselves into areas where they are not welcome.

For our own students, we provide a list of places not to use and things not to do:

Do not:

- Go on the roofs (they are flat and accessible, so this needs spelling out);
- Go to the caretaker's house;
- Use dark areas behind the stage;
- Go on the railway line at the back of the college;
- Make noise in corridors;
- Borrow knives from the canteen;
- Splash ketchup anywhere.

Every year the list gets longer as ingenious students think up somewhere else to go and someone else complains ...

Off the premises we make it clear that they are not to simulate in any public place any activity which might be construed as illegal. For example, pretend guns and sacks of white powder might be obvious props to them, but this is not always the case with passers-by who don't spot the camera. Nor do they have our permission to film anything dangerous (car chases, hanging off tall buildings, lying on railway lines, driving over the camera etc). We have found the local police very helpful for student projects and have no wish to antagonise them – they have often shown willingness to let our students be 'banged up' in their cells, for filmic purposes.

Loan of equipment

The insurance position on equipment loaned to students is a grey area; it is important to institute a system which ensures that you know exactly which equipment has been loaned to which students and for how long. During big projects you may lend out as many as a dozen cameras overnight. Each camera needs charged batteries, the correct tape and completed paperwork. We put stickers on the outside of the camera bag so that we know when it is ready, which group is collecting it, what time they are coming and what time they are bringing it back.

Any group borrowing a camera has to have a loan letter signed by the parent of one of the group, which is exchanged for the camera and kept on file. (A sample letter is provided at www.bfi.org.uk/tfms.) The letter probably has no legal status, but seems to work in 'moral' terms. You must keep students to their obligations in terms of cameras being returned on time. We are prepared to deduct marks from the planning component if they are late back with a camera and students are told this in advance; it seems to work as they are rarely late back.

● Editing

What equipment do you need?

In the past, Centres offering video work on a low-to-medium budget moved from in-camera editing to two machine assembly or insert editing, usually with only one or two set-ups, shared between many students on a rolling basis. The shift to digital means that it is possible to have multiple set-ups, where students can do much more with ease and where they can have access on a more regular basis. As suggested for cameras, it is better to have more equipment for regular access than fewer machines with rare access.

Where to buy

Again not from your local ICT superstore. Try education departments of main dealers. Buy computer magazines and trawl through the display adverts and, as with cameras, compare prices and get at least three parallel quotes.

Peripherals

● One of the most useful items to buy is an external hard drive, which allows you to move large files off the computer either prior to putting them onto video or while someone else uses the machine. A FireWire external hard drive with 40GB can be purchased for less than £300 and effectively gives you the storage capacity of another computer. The latest models are no bigger than a slab of chocolate and can fit in your pocket. They are also very fast.

- The usual printers and scanners are needed for any multimedia set-up but if your main work is DV editing, you don't need them dedicated to every machine.
- A Zip drive, to transfer graphics files, is also useful.
- If you have analogue cameras, which you need to continue using, it is possible to buy an analogue to digital converter such as the Formac Studio.

Mac or PC?

The type of computer that you buy is often dictated by your whole school or college requirements; to this end PCs are often chosen, as in most schools PCs predominate. However, using a PC as an editing suite can cause problems, as you need to make sure that it has a FireWire port to import the footage, a suitable video card and a suitable sound card. It is worth remembering that not all PCs have this equipment, which can add to the cost of a machine.

All recent iMacs, eMacs and G4s come with this equipment as standard and tend to be a much more stable platform for video and graphics work. They also come with iMovie as standard, which means that you do not have to buy more editing software; at the time of writing this is still the most straightforward package to use, ideal for students and teachers new to DV editing.

Another problem is the common insistence in schools that the PCs must be networked for other uses, because you need ideally at least 40GB of storage space for DV projects (see below). The majority of Macs come with 40GB of hard disk space and in some cases 60GB. This means that a number of groups can use one machine in rotation and that projects do not need to be removed from the machine with as much haste as they might if the machine had a smaller hard disk. Apple have a range of educational machines, which are called eMacs, and have educational dealers who are increasingly expert at understanding the needs of Media Studies departments.

In many cases you may have no choice, so if you do go down the PC route make sure you have advisors you can trust. An integral video capture card is essential, and if you want to continue using existing analogue cameras, you will need to buy one which allows analogue input. The most commonly used cards are Pinnacle and Matrox, which can include FireWire and analogue inputs and outputs, but you need to check compatibility with your computer.

Microsoft are about to release an edit program (Movie Maker 2 for Windows XP, available currently in a well-reviewed beta version on the internet) which may give PCs the edge for entry-level DV. The first version of the program, advertised extensively on the release of the XP system, was widely seen as too limited but the second version appears to have many advantages in terms of both importing and exporting file formats.

Standalone or network?

The demands made by any edit program will put a massive strain on a network unless it is specifically designed for video work. Such work will slow down a network and lead to crashes; in addition you lose control of your machines – some maintenance of the system is needed when you are undertaking a lot of video work, and you don't want to have to keep running to your IT support staff to do this for you. In addition there is likely to be the problem of file sharing; video files are very big and students are unlikely to be allocated sufficient space on a school/college system. If the system is PC-based and you want to run Macs, then you have to have some very good and willing technicians to get it all to work. Even if it is all PC-based, the particular Windows operating system may find it hard to cope with programs like Adobe Premiere.

● **Editing software**

As with cameras there are more and more editing programs available. While the actual software that you choose will be influenced by your computer system and your budget, you should remember that usability is the key feature. Another consideration is whether you are able to have a dedicated digital editing suite, which can use more complex software, or whether your computers are used for other purposes and are networked throughout the school or college, in which case you will probably have to use less complex software.

The most commonly used editing programs are:

- Apple iMovie (Macs only)
- Adobe Premiere (PCs and Macs)
- Apple Final Cut Pro (Macs only)
- Media 100 (PCs and Macs)

Each of these has its advantages and disadvantages (and devotees), and these will be discussed later. There are a number of things that you should consider when choosing editing software. These include:

- **Interface** – Most editing software uses a similar interface; it should be easy to navigate with enough timelines for both the audio and video channels.
- **Video capturing** – Not all programs capture software in the same way, for example iMovie automatically breaks the footage into smaller 'chunks' and stores this on its 'shelf'. Other programs require manual capture of the clips, which is often time-consuming but does give you complete control over what is imported.
- **RAM** – Some programs need more RAM to run effectively; this is especially true at the higher end of the spectrum. Première and Final Cut Pro both need at least 256MB to work effectively, possibly more for later versions.

Editing software is becoming increasingly easy to use, but you should make sure that you are happy using the technology and there are a number of useful reference books available.

Apple iMovie

Undoubtedly the biggest breakthrough for digital editing in media education came with the advent of Apple's iMovie program in 1999, which now comes free with every iMac. It is Apple's entry-level program, ideal for domestic users and beginners, and it is extremely easy to use, with an intuitive interface. You can get into the tutorial straight away and there are some excellent resources around to assist in its use. In Unit 3 you will find examples of tasks and induction work with iMovie.

Advantages
- Excellent for beginners;
- Intuitive interface;
- Reasonable menu of features;
- Instant rendering;
- Free with i/eMacs/G4s.

Disadvantages
- Only available on Macs;
- Limited range of features compared to other programs;
- Only one video timeline and two audio;
- Matching sound to image (eg lip synch) a matter of trial and error;
- Limited captioning options.

(However, iMovie3 has enhanced features, especially for sound)

Adobe Premiere

This is probably the most popular program and runs on both Macs and PCs. It comes from the same suite of products as Adobe Illustrator and Adobe Photoshop, so shares similar features in its interface. It is quite complex to learn initially but it does have a number of advantages once you have grasped the basics. While a lot of teachers have experienced problems with it, posted to internet message boards, these seem mainly to be a result of its initial configuration or their lack of knowledge. With proper training and configuration, however, there is no reason for such problems. However, it does illustrate the need for advance preparation.

With a PC you still need to purchase a compatible video card and either print directly to VHS or export to DV tape using the DV-in function on a digital video camera.

Advantages
- Relatively inexpensive for licences (£80 per machine);
- Lots of features, including 'Chromakey';
- Audio waves mean matching sound and vision is possible;
- Multiple audio and video tracks.

Disadvantages
- Initially complex to use;
- Program must be set up properly;
- Needs 256MB of RAM to work well;
- A PC will need a separate video card, though it will work on any Mac with FireWire;
- Needs a well-structured induction course and lots of teacher expertise.

Apple Final Cut Pro

Final Cut Pro is Apple's top-end editing program; it can only be used on Macs and the Mac has to meet certain system requirements before it can be used.

Final Cut Pro 3 requires:

- Mac OS X v10.1.1 or Mac OS 9.2.2 (operating systems);
- A Mac with a 300MHz or faster PowerPC G3 or G4 processor with built-in FireWire, 256MB of RAM (384MB recommended for G4 real-time effects) and 40MB of available disk space for installation;
- A 500MHz (or higher) PowerPC G4 processor is required for G4 real-time effects;
- A 667MHz PowerBook G4 is required for mobile real-time DV effects.

However Final Cut Pro is the most powerful editing program in its price range and is suitable for either the professional or amateur user. You should use Final Cut Pro only if you are technically competent or have experience with other editing programs. It is also more expensive than other packages around but in part this is due to its capabilities, which are greater than Adobe Première. Given the wealth of features available in Final Cut Pro it is likely that the majority of users follow the 80/20 rule in that they use 20% of the features 80% of the time and the other 80% of the features 20% of the time. It is worth buying a quick reference book as the Final Cut Pro manual is very thick and detailed.

Advantages

- Powerful editing package, commonly used by professionals;
- Recognisable interface;
- Wealth of features including colour correction tools;
- Real-time rendering (dependent on system);
- Experienced users will get fantastic results;
- Offers excellent progression for able students wishing to take a Media or Film Studies degree (and will impress HE admissions tutors) or work in media production.

Disadvantages

- Expensive;
- Difficult for the novice user;
- Macintosh OS only, does not work on PCs;
- Needs top-end Macs for best results;
- Needs close teacher guidance (you need to know how to use it).

Overall Final Cut Pro offers the closest experience to professional editing of any of the packages. Apple have just released Final Cut Express, a 'lite' version of the program, which is substantially cheaper but offers all the features an educational user might require.

Media 100

Up until the emergence of the semi-pro market (Final Cut Pro and Premiere), Media 100 was the only software to compete with AVID's hold as the industry standard digital editing package. Media 100 software was built to run on the Apple Mac, but there is a PC version called I-Finish DV.

The step up to the professional software gives you multiple timeline and bin options as well as a more stable working environment. Geared towards those using other effects and graphics packages, it is billed by the company as a content creation system. The interface is thus uncomplicated and user-friendly in comparison to Final Cut Pro or Premiere. Most of the editing functions are easily located in the tool bar with an easy-to-use shortcut system, which suits both regular users and those unfamiliar with graphics software.

Requirements
- 300MHz or faster PowerPC G3 or G4 processor/300MHz PC;
- DV FireWire (costly upgrade for analogue compatibility).

Advantages
- Simple interface, accessible for inexperienced users;
- Very quick handling for regular user (suits keyboard shortcuts);

- Very stable;
- Real-time preview of motion and colour effects;
- Multiple timeline and bin options;
- Audio wave form display;
- Ideal for accessing clips or sections of edited footage between projects or timelines.

Disadvantages

- Very expensive: Media 100 is available in several versions with varying limitations – basic versions are priced around £2000;
- Projects, timelines and bins are saved separately making filing hazardous for inexperienced users;
- Limited in-built titling and effects (most editors use with either After Effect or Borris effect packages);
- Limited audio and video tracks;
- Non-expandable preview and editing window.

Organising and storing work

Probably the most crucial thing when dealing with large numbers of students is ensuring all work is organised and stored so that nothing gets mislaid. It is vital to set up your machines with folders which correspond to teaching groups to ensure that everyone knows where they should save their work.

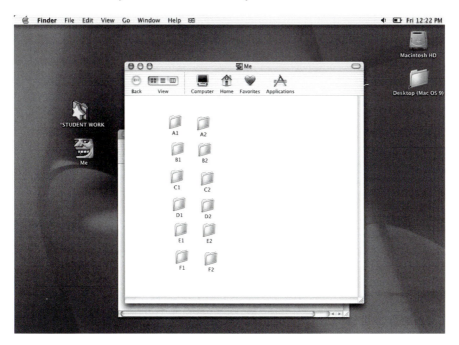

Our system of organisation involves setting up a folder for each task with an appropriate identifying icon. Inside this folder is a sub-folder for each teaching group. Since only one group from any one class will work on a particular machine, then anything stored in that folder will be by that group. This ensures work is accessible and instantly retrievable. Since introducing this system we have had a 99% success rate in appropriate filing (compared to about 10% when we had just one or two machines and students were left to file work themselves). Students must be taken through the filing system during induction to ensure that they are able to use it effectively.

● Tape archives

Since finished student work will need to be accessible for a range of reasons, including for moderation purposes, students' own showreels, and examples of work to show to future classes and on open evenings, it is very important to keep accurately labelled archives. We have a master DV tape for every class which contains all the work of that class throughout the year, from induction activities through to finished AS or A2 projects. We also produce a VHS copy for classroom use and additionally a compilation DV and VHS tape from each project containing all the work of the year group. We are now beginning to produce DVD compilations, which should make instant access and playback even easier.

● Thinking ahead

The archive of finished work is important, but so is planning ahead. You need to ensure that every group has a tape to shoot on and that nothing is accidentally erased by another group. We buy a big stock of DV tapes at the start of the year and label them, with six for each teaching group during the induction period. Thus, for example, only a student in Group C1 using Camera 1 will have recorded anything on the tape C1/1 (provided we haven't loaded it up wrongly).

For later projects, every group is given its own unique number (for example, from 1 to 60) and there is a file on their machine, within the project folder and teaching group folder, labelled with that unique number. The group's tape is also labelled with that number, so no work should go astray. When projects are completed, tapes are recycled and renumbered.

The same process of planning ahead is important in terms of storage space on the machines. For example, if your computers only have 10GB of storage space each, it is quickly eaten up when there are several groups of students using the machines to save material for their projects. It is thus essential to set a working limit for students importing material so that the hard drive is not filled too quickly. If five groups are using a machine then something in the region of

1.5GB (or about eight minutes of footage) ought to be the maximum saved. There is no real need on small projects such as adverts or title sequences for students to keep significantly more raw footage on the machine as they can always import from the tape at the start of their next session. The bigger the hard drive the more material can be saved, though it is worth bearing in mind that the machine's performance will be less effective the more full it is.

A note on technical support

Just as a Science department cannot function without equipment and technicians, neither can a Media department. As in a Science lab, in the Media department it is important for the teacher to have a good understanding of equipment and software. There is a tendency in Media Studies for teachers to split courses between the experts on 'theory' and on 'practical' work, which demonstrates a lack of understanding of what students are being asked to do in each part of the course. We would advocate a more holistic approach with all teachers participating in all areas of the course, accepting that they will bring different levels of expertise to different areas.

In our college, where we have almost 600 students taking our courses, we rely on technical support within the department for the day-to-day organisation of equipment and for longer-term development of technology. We have the equivalent of a full-time technician, justified only by our large cohort. All staff are timetabled for practical lessons, with some requiring more technical back-up than others.

We would not advocate reliance upon central IT support unless it is the only option. Technicians in most schools' central IT systems only deal with specific problems relating to the network, and are not expected to assist students, which is what a Media department needs. In most institutions central IT support is also unlikely to be able to provide expertise with particular programs or platforms (especially for Mac users). You may need to teach yourself to troubleshoot and to acquire increasing long-term support based on student numbers. With video editing in iMovie most problems can be solved by anyone with a few months of Mac use behind them. Hardware problems are rare and cannot usually be solved by an in-house technician anyway, so the machine should be sent back to the dealer.

3

Hands on

In this unit, we provide:

- Outlines for two induction programmes for shooting and editing short films, using Apple iMovie and Adobe Première;
- A list of basic pre- and post-production principles, including storyboarding, that students should be made aware of;
- Guidelines on the management of students during the shooting and editing process;
- Recommendations on the post-production assessment processes;
- An outline for a bigger project – the making of a music video.

Digital video induction routes

• Route 1: Apple iMovie

An induction programme needs to be stepped developmentally so that students learn one stage at a time and can build up their skills. The assumption of this induction programme is that they will have no previous experience of video camera use or editing, nor of Media Studies key concepts or the systematic analysis of moving image texts.

We have designed ten practical sessions which build up skills and culminate in an equipment 'driving test' to see how well students are able to use the equipment on their own. Each session lasts roughly an hour and the ten should be run in parallel with ten sessions of equal length that focus on theoretical and analytical work, some of which could mesh with the practical sessions by involving analysis of the finished induction exercises.

The digital 'driving test' has been developed to prepare students adequately before they even start to think about any assessed video production work. Too often, experience of moderating students' work nationally demonstrates that the piece submitted for assessment represents the student's first attempt at video and, inevitably, the marks awarded (at least by the moderator) reflect this. No-one should be expected to get it right first time!

In our case, we have a full suite of iMacs (enough for students to work in pairs in timetabled lessons) but the activities outlined here could be adapted for other contexts with fewer machines, either by working in groups of four and rotating whose hands control the mouse, or by running a carousel of activities with some groups on the computers and some on the cameras. The latter is more complex to organise but is the way we operated before we went digital.

Digital driving lessons

In the first two sessions, students are shown the computer filing system and do exercises with Adobe Photoshop to acquire basic skills, which they will be using later in the course.

Session 1 – Adobe Photoshop

In Session 1, take a photo of each student (using a digital still camera or a digital video camera with a still function) and import it onto the computer so the students can manipulate it and add text (their own names). This is also useful as you get a full set of class photos to match up to the register.

Session 2 – Adobe Photoshop

Give students an image bank of material to work with, using Photoshop's many graphic effects, filters and treatments, from which they have to construct a flyer for an imaginary club. This image bank can be put together from scans of interesting pictures and postcards, or images downloaded from the web, or picked up free with cover-mounted CD-ROMs from computer magazines. This task immediately produces striking results suitable for display. It also introduces a few Photoshop effects which can be used in early iMovie sessions.

Session 3 – *Picture Power*

Students undertake their first editing task, using the English and Media Centre's CD-ROM resource *Picture Power* (which comes with its own accessible instructions) to construct a sequence of still images which tell a story (**Worksheet 1**). The task is to produce a complete sequence of 'Pursued' with a soundtrack. They can add sound and transitions. The completed task is saved under the students' names in the teaching group folder located in the *Picture Power* folder on the desktop and played back at the end of the session, when all members of the class can circulate and look at each other's work.

worksheet ① *Picture Power* task

Your task is to produce a complete sequence of 'Pursued' with soundtrack, to play back at the end of the session.

• Insert the **Picture Power** disk.
• Double click on the **Picture Power** icon on the desktop.
• Double click 'Pursued'.
• By moving images onto the image track you can construct a sequence of stills to tell the story in different ways. You can add sound and transitions.
• See the information with the CD for further details.
• When you complete the task save it under your name in your teaching group folder located in the **Picture Power** folder in 'Student Work'.

Page 1 of 1   Digital Video Production

This task is a useful introduction to editing as part of the process of storytelling in that there is no shooting to be done, no moving images to cut up and only a minimal number of effects to choose from. It nonetheless simulates the whole process of digital editing and future exercises can be built upon it. Above all, it draws attention to the constructed nature of storytelling and starts to introduce the forms and conventions of camerawork, which will be essential in all student video work.

Session 4 – iMovie Tutorial

Here we move another step forward by introducing iMovie. In preparation you need to load copies of the iMovie tutorial into each group's folder on every machine as once one copy of the tutorial is altered and saved, it is impossible to restore it to the original footage.

After providing a brief demonstration, using a digital projector so the whole class can see, of the basic features of the program (how to drop clips onto the timeline, how to cut a clip, the transition, titles, audio and effects menus), ask students to undertake a version of the tutorial in which they play around with every menu and with the supplied tutorial footage (a 'cheesy' sequence involving two cute American kids washing a dog) to construct a film which lasts exactly 30 seconds (**Worksheet 2**).

The film should include material from all six clips as well as at least three different transitions, three different titles and three different sound clips. Students may also try out slow motion, backwards footage or effects such as sepia tinting. The idea is to make them familiar with the interface and able to complete a task in a limited time.

This activity introduces the manipulation of existing moving images. It also gives them the opportunity to be a bit silly. This is essential early on, to get as much comedy out of their systems as possible, otherwise they will carry on being silly no matter what exercises they are set. Again the session ends with an opportunity for all students to circulate and see each other's results.

Session 5 – Shooting video: 'Horror stills'

Now students finally get to use the cameras. However, they are only allowed to shoot still images which they will sequence within iMovie in session 6, limiting the new complications introduced by the exercise.

The session begins with a teacher demonstration of the camera's main functions (on/off, record/pause, still function, zoom) and of how to attach it safely to the tripod. All groups then have to demonstrate that they can operate the camera and tripod, before they are allowed out of the classroom to start the task. This is called 'Horror stills', in which students shoot some stills to make up an imaginary horror film. Students are given strict instructions on where they can and cannot go and, as much as anything, the exercise is a test of how well they can be trusted with equipment outside the classroom. They have to make between ten and twelve stills which they will edit in the second session. (**Worksheet 3 – Session 1**) They then come back to the classroom and download the stills into iMovie, saving the work ready for next time.

Session 6 – Editing the stills

For this session, you will need to provide horror film or thriller soundtracks, which are easily available on CD. Students will edit the shots they have taken into a thirty second sequence, adding transitions, captions and sound effects, all to a soundtrack of thirty seconds from an existing horror film or thriller. They can export their stills to Photoshop to add gory effects or dismemberments which would not be possible with moving shots in iMovie alone.

These two sessions build on the earlier ones conceptually, but also extend student skills into using the camera and downloading footage into iMovie. This

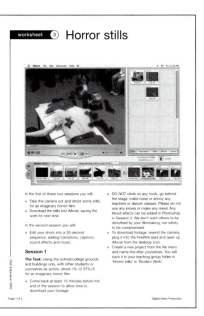

is an accessible and fun way to start, from what students already know about the codes and conventions of a horror film. (**Worksheet 3 – Session 2**). Later, for more sustained projects, it is important that students study the codes and conventions of existing media texts in the course of planning their own. Unlike previous sessions, however, there is not simply a tour round to view at the end of the editing session; this time the finished films are exported to tape and used in a follow-up lesson, as material to screen and analyse. You should also offer a critique of the techniques students used.

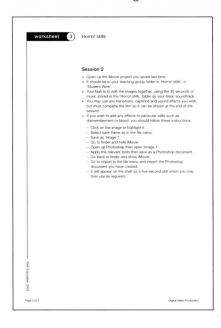

Session 7 & 8 – Shooting video footage: *the phone call*

These sessions involve students shooting a sequence of moving images which they have to edit together. However, unlike the Horror stills task where a lot of creative freedom was allowed in composing images, this task is very strictly organised around a sequence of shots in a particular order. The aim is for students to learn about cross-cutting, framing, shot composition and distance, and to gain a better understanding of the scope and limitations of the camera (particularly where sound is concerned, since it involves dialogue).

The activity comprises filming a phone call, since the one thing you can guarantee most students will have at their disposal is a mobile phone. The students are asked to use two different locations and are also given a worksheet (**Worksheet 4 – Session 1**), which contains a shooting sequence and instructions for each shot, and a paper **clapperboard**. Session 7 ends with them importing their footage into iMovie. In session 8 (**Worksheet 4 – Session 2**), they have the task of cutting their material to make a complete phone call, so that the edited version makes sense.

---

worksheet ④ **The phone call**

In the first of these two sessions you will.

• Take out the camera in a small group and shoot a sequence.
• Return and download the stills into iMovie, saving the work for next time.

In the second session you will.

• Edit your shots to create a short sequence.

Session 1: Shooting the sequence

Take out the camera and shoot the following sequence precisely according to the directions below (it would be sensible to use a clapperboard to number each shot).

1. Establishing shot of the setting;
2. Medium shot of character 1 (facing left);
3. Close up of character 1 taking out mobile phone;
4. Close up of mobile phone being dialled;
5. Profile shot of character waiting for phone to connect (facing left);
6. Medium frontal shot of character speaking on phone;
7. Profile shot of same (facing left);
8. Close up of character's mouth as she/he says goodbye;
9. Medium shot of character 2 in different setting;
10. Close shot of character 2 reaction to phone ringing (facing right);
11. Close shot of phone;
12. Close shot of character 2 picking up phone;
13. Medium shot of character 2 responding to call, from front;
14. Same shot from side (facing right);
15. Close-up of character 2 saying goodbye;
16. Long shot of character putting away the phone.

You should pay close attention to shot distance, angle, framing and catching the dialogue. In the next session you will edit the footage together to tell the whole story.

Your teacher may supply you with a set of clapperboard sheets for 16 shots, collated into a ring binder. At the start of each shot hold the clapperboard with the relevant shot number in front of the camera, so that each shot is clearly labelled.

Page 1 of 2   Digital Video Production

---

worksheet ④ The phone call

Session 2: Editing the footage

In this session you are to edit your footage to enable the viewer to see and hear the conversation between the characters.

• If you used the clapperboard, then the job of finding each of the sixteen shots will be easier. You will need to trim each shot and remove the clapperboard.

• You are asked to edit the sequence in the following way:

Shots 1–3, 9, 4, 10, 5, 11, 12, 6, 13, 7, 14, 8, 15, 16.

• You should use only one title at the beginning, and at the end you may include credits. Try to use only cuts and no other transitions. Do not use any sound effects, but try to cut the sequence so that your original sound works as well as possible.

The sequence must be finished this lesson.

Page 2 of 2   Digital Video Production

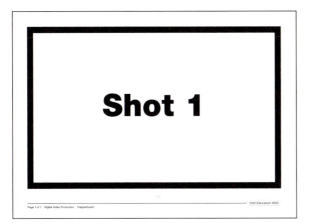

Shot 1

Page 1 of 1 Digital Video Production Clapperboard   ©b6 Education 2003

This paper clapperboard consists of 16 sheets (Shot 1 – Shot 16). The sheets can be photocopied – one set for each group – and inserted in a ring binder. During shooting, the clpapperboard with the relevant shot number can be held in front of the camera at the start of each shot.

Session 9 – De-brief and evaluation

As with the Horror stills activity, the finished efforts are put on video tape and analysed in another session. What these exercises reveal is that there is still an awful long way for students to go; they make every mistake it is possible to make, from switching off the camera too quickly and losing vital dialogue to filming at too great a distance so dialogue is inaudible. Nonetheless, a tremendous amount of learning is going on and in future work, huge improvements are evident as a result of learning from the mistakes here.

Session 10 – the 'driving test'

The last session of the induction course involves the 'driving test' (**Worksheet 5**), where students come into the room individually and have to undertake a set of basic tasks, including mounting the camera on the tripod, shooting footage, importing it into iMovie and doing some basic editing, watched by a member of staff. Though there is no pass or fail line, any of the tasks they are unable to do they are shown again.

The aim of these sessions is to avoid a situation where one member of a group always defers to another in the practical project, so never actually learns how to use the equipment. This way we at least ensure that all students can use the equipment, which isn't always possible to tell in the pace of the classroom.

Most of the activities in this induction could be adapted easily for use with other programs, though we would argue that most programs would take several sessions of induction rather than the one which is needed for iMovie. The *bfi* report on the BECTA digital video editing project suggests that iMovie might be seen as insufficient for Key Stage 4 and above:

> 'Some teachers and a small number of pupils commented that while iMovie 2 is a very good interface for introducing editing of DV footage in a user-friendly way, it has some limitations when exploring moving image production recursively or in greater depth, as for example in the media studies curriculum at Key Stage 4 and beyond. This has implications for advanced learners who, for example, may need more scope to edit soundtracks on a greater number of separate timelines. There are many

other DVE packages that offer these features and it would be useful to consider which of these might serve as a useful 'step-up' from iMovie 2 for those pupils who begin to encounter limitation'. (p.28)

Our experience is that the small number of students we inherit at A level who have been lucky enough to learn digital editing at GCSE in Media Studies have learnt on more sophisticated packages such as Premiere and Media 100 and do appear a bit 'sniffy' about iMovie at first; however, many quickly find that their apparent skills with DV editing are quickly outstripped by novices on an apparently inferior program.

It is the case, however, that once students begin to stretch the potential of the program, there are some things they just cannot do, so we do offer a brief introduction to titling in Premiere in Term 2 of the AS course (Year 12), to allow a more sophisticated 'finish' to the second piece of coursework. In Term 3 we do a full-scale Premiere induction ready for the A2 practical project (Year 13). Our recommendation would be to hold back on introducing programs like Première however until you feel fully confident of your students' competence, as we still find that at A2 some of the best projects are produced on iMovie.

The sessions using Premiere which follow are undertaken by our students at the end of the AS course, before commencing A2.

● **Route 2: Adobe Premiere**

As with the iMovie programme, this induction programme is stepped developmentally so that students learn one stage at a time and can build up their skills. The aim is to provide students with a clear idea of how the program works and the extra features that it has. Though this induction is used after the students are familiar with iMovie, it could also be used if the students have no experience of non-linear editing software, which could be an advantage. The course is based on our experience but is not meant to be prescriptive; in fact it is likely that it would need to be adapted for different groups of students.

There are seven sessions that focus on different elements of the program and continually develop the students' skills base so that they are constantly reusing techniques in order to become comfortable with them. However the course does not cover the more technical aspects of using Premiere. This is best learnt by attending a course or by using the program. It is important that you are familiar with the program as students are likely to ask questions about it which are beyond the material covered here. There are many good manuals that cover Premiere in some detail and once you know the program it is not that difficult to use.

To be successful, these sessions require a large input from you: you will need to collect footage and music tracks to be used as source material, adapted from existing sources (mainly previous student raw footage), so there is no need for students to shoot and import new footage. All material should be ready on the hard drives at the start of the course. This planning makes the course easier and allows each session to be completed in an hour. We produced a booklet on the key features of Premiere, adapted from the manual and our experience of using the program, so that the students had an individual point of reference as well as following it via data projection.

Session 1 – Setting up a new video project: using the interface

This session introduces the students to the program. You first need to explain the following:

- How to set up a new project and what project settings to use;
- The terms used so that they are aware of why as well as how to do something;
- How Premiere saves files – this is very important as students who fail to file their work correctly can cause problems for themselves and others. The program may fail to find files or find unwanted material from another group's work, causing crashes and even the loss of projects. You need to stress how important it is to make a project file and how this works.

After these important preliminaries you need to introduce the interface. It is important to demystify this early on, as it can look complex. You need to explain the basic functions that students will need to know, beginning with how to import a single file and how it will appear in the interface. Students then import a whole folder into their project and then save the project.

Set them a straightforward task of reconstructing a short film, which has been cut up into different clips, out of order. To make this task easier you can give the students an order in which to reassemble the clips, so that it becomes a jigsaw that they have to piece together (with a genuine right answer). The idea of this task is to reinforce students' new skills as it only uses the tools they have been taught.

Session 2 – Editing video and audio clips

This session builds upon the skills from session 1. You need to show students the various ways of editing clips. Their task is to put together a short sequence from the clips provided, using an audio file you have chosen and placed in the folder. This allows students to start cutting or fading to the tempo of a given piece of music.

Sessions 3 & 4 – Lip-synching

Lip-synching is a technique used for the music video project that the students undertake at A2. Students need to import into their folders footage of a band playing together with the appropriate audio track, then you need to show them how to add more tracks to the timeline. When they have placed the footage on the timeline, show them the purpose of the synch mode and how to use it.

Set students the task of lip-synching the performance and the audio track; and show them how to line up a couple of clips. The rest of the session and session 4 are spent constructing a short video, which allows the students to reinforce their skills. This is a useful tool to understand and will be used in other projects.

Session 5 – Using transitions and effects

This session you need to cover transitions and some of the effects available in Adobe Première. After inserting a number of transitions, students then start adding effects to the clips in the timeline. There are a large number of these available and some are better than others. You should encourage students to experiment and use a number of different effects so that they have a clear idea of what is possible within Premiere. This also helps to differentiate the program from iMovie. Show students how to preview the effects before rendering them. The ability to do this saves time as it prevents them applying effects only to realise that they are not appropriate for their project. This is an advantage Premiere has over a less complex program such as iMovie. Students should make notes about the interesting effects and transitions.

Session 6 – Animation of still images and titles

In this session you introduce students to the motion settings which allow them to animate still images and titles through importing other file types, in this case Adobe Photoshop files, and mixing them with moving images. The basic steps are as follows:

- Import a Photoshop file of an object such as a plane, and drag it onto the timeline. In Premiere a still image can be stretched to any length.
- Arrange the clips on the timeline so that the still image is overlaying the moving clips.
- Show students how to use the transparency settings in Premiere.
- Once the image has been successfully overlaid, show students how to apply motion to the still image to make it move through the frame. This gives the impression that it is moving with the clip. This particular process is fairly technical and rather than go into detail it would be best to consult a 'how to' manual on Premiere.
- Show students how to add extra images and also how to add other moving clips into the timeline.
- Once this has been mastered, show students how else the transparency tool can be used to add effects such as scratches over the top of clips and how the motion tool can be used to create camera movements. This last tool is particularly useful as it gives the impression of a controlled track rather than a zoom. As with any effect though it needs to be carefully used or it can appear messy.

Session 7 – Creating titles

In this session you can cover the use of titles and recap the techniques that have been used in other sessions. Though adding titles in Premiere is fairly simple, making them stand out is harder to do. By carefully using the techniques students can produce professional-looking titles. It is also possible to design titles in Adobe Photoshop, import these as still clips into Premiere and add motion to make them move. This compensates for the limitations of titling in Premiere.

Basic principles

To enable students to manage their projects you need to make sure they understand the importance of certain principles. These include:

- Pre-production, including the preparation of storyboards;
- Shooting, including camera techniques, sound and lighting and content issues;
- Editing.

● Pre-production

● They need to do focused research: it doesn't matter how many examples of real media texts they study, so long as they really *see and understand* what they are looking at. If they are making TV advertisements, they need to break down some real adverts to see how they are shot and edited. If they are making thriller openings they need to look at tapes of some real examples and identify their key features and how they are put together. They need to concentrate on formal and technical aspects – these are just as important as content, if not more so.

● They need to plan and organise down to the tiniest detail: where they will be shooting, who is going to be there, what they will be wearing, who will bring the props, what time everyone will meet up, what each shot is going to look like. They should make a simple shooting log – and make sure everyone involved has a copy.

---

student notes — Video shoot shot list

Here is an example of a shot list for video shoots. On the next page is a blank shot list for your to photocopy.
● Include sufficient details from your storyboard ideas, as a quick reference when preparing for a shoot or on location.
● Make sure everyone has a copy, to be retained as planning evidence.

Shot No.	Shot/framing etc.	Action	Info (costumes, props, locations, personnel etc)
1	CU	Person, phone in hand, sending message	Phone, outdoors
2	MS	Person looks annoyed with phone	Phone, outdoors. John, red jacket
3	MS	Male figure approaching to speak	Danny with blue cap
4	LS	Computer room door opens	Room C116, John
5			
6			
7			
8			
9			
10			

Page 1 of 2 — Digital Video Production

---

template — Video shoot shot list

Group members:
Project title:
Teacher:

Shot Number	Shot/Framing etc.	Action	Info (costumes, props, locations, personnel etc)

Page 2 of 2 — Digital Video Production

● For group work, they should take down each other's mobile phone numbers right from the start. They should agree to phone each other straight away if there are any problems or if anyone fails to show up. It must be stressed that students who are frequently absent let other members of the group down; they therefore cannot expect to pick up marks for the process. All members of the group are expected to pull their weight at all times; they will not be credited if they are not a fully active member of the group.

- They must not waste any time. If someone is absent, they should improvise. There is no way anyone should say they can't do anything because someone absent has the storyboards – they are *all* responsible. They should always have a back-up plan – what happens if it is raining?
- In group work there are often arguments on how to do things. The rule should be: simplest is best. Never try to make things more complicated. Keep it simple, do it well. The more complex the idea, the more can go wrong. Complex film openings run the risk of being confusing for the audience.
- Whatever the deadline, they should set themselves a deadline of a week earlier, that way they allow for any unexpected mishaps.
- They should never shoot anything until they have a storyboard or shot list. They can always change this plan on the shoot, but without a plan, they will shoot rubbish – guaranteed!
- They should always create original images unless there really is no alternative (such as needing an explosion, where it is clearly more sensible to get one off a tape). Dressing up fellow students or teachers or even parents as characters for their work is much more effective than using footage of real actors taken from elsewhere.
- If they need some music, they should make sure they can get it early on in the project – not leaving it to teachers to find at the last minute. Local libraries often have a very good stock of CDs which can be borrowed for a small fee. And they shouldn't use the most obvious tracks – everyone else will be using them too!
- Before they start a project, students should look at examples of previous students' work; identify their strengths and their weaknesses – they can build on the former and avoid the latter. But they should beware of criticising this work too loudly or negatively as their own will be available for next year's students to look at and by then they'll have realised that professional-looking work is not as easy to produce after all. They should use previous student work to identify clichés to avoid, such as endless *Blair Witch*-style rip-offs.
- They should double check that batteries are fully charged before they go on location and avoid using the LCD as it runs the battery down very quickly and always have a spare or a charger.
- They must take care of all equipment entrusted to them; cameras to be taken off the premises overnight will only be issued on receipt of the required form signed by a parent. Any damage or loss MUST be reported on return.

Storyboarding

The following section introduces storyboarding and its key role in the pre-production process. Another title in this series, *Teaching Scriptwriting, Screenplays and Storyboards for Film and TV Production* by Mark Readman, provides guidelines for developing students' skills in this area which will help improve the quality of their project.

What is a storyboard?

A storyboard is a series of sequential drawings or pictures that are used to represent the intended shots in the film. Ideally the storyboard will be a paper version of the finished film. It shows how the filmmaker intends to shoot and frame various shots, and illustrates camera movements that will be used. It also shows how a number of shots are going to link together to form a scene. Often finished storyboards can resemble a comic or graphic novel without the voice bubbles. A completed storyboard should allow anyone to have a clear idea of how shots will work and link together.

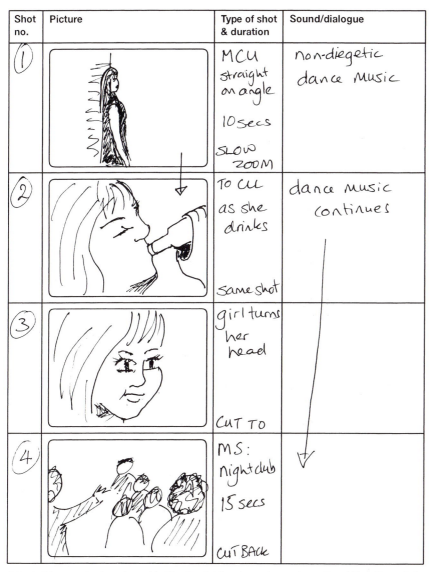

Shot no.	Picture	Type of shot & duration	Sound/dialogue
①		MCU straight on angle 10 secs SLOW ZOOM	non-diegetic dance music
②		TO CU as she drinks same shot	dance music continues
③		girl turns her head CUT TO	
④		MS: nightclub 15 secs CUT BACK	

Adapted from a storyboard provided by Sarah Mannix, student at Long Road Sixth Form College.

Why storyboard?

Storyboarding is an excellent starting point for any filmmaker, allowing them to put down ideas on paper and think about what they want to achieve. It also helps them to communicate their ideas more clearly to other people involved in the process. Few filmmakers will make a film without some form of storyboard to aid them; this can vary from rough scribbles to immaculate and detailed artwork, it all depends on the filmmaker's needs. An excellent example of filmmakers who use storyboards are the Coen brothers.

> 'Storyboarding has always been an important part of figuring out how to do a movie.'   (Joel Coen, quoted in Robertson and Cooke, 1998)

Joel and Ethan Coen storyboard the whole film before shooting it. This is often the way low-budget filmmakers work as it allows them to visualise all the shots and work out precisely what is needed and avoid unnecessary shots that will increase the budget. Storyboarding the whole film first allows the Coens to communicate their ideas quickly to the crew. For instance in *The Big Lebowski* (1998) there are less than 20 shots that were not originally storyboarded.

What about drawing skills?

Drawing skills are not important. A storyboard does not need to be a work of art; it simply allows filmmakers the opportunity to experiment on paper, which is cheap, rather than on film, which is expensive. It provides the opportunity to work through a number of ideas before committing them to film (even though DV tape is cheaper than film it is still more expensive than paper). As for the quality of drawings, the only thing to avoid is stick figures as these give no sense of how a person will fill the frame; rough outlines of figures are fine.

Moving images

A storyboard is made up of still images but it needs to show how the movement in a finished film will work. There are a number of ways of adding movement to still pictures. The most common way is by using arrows; for example, to show a pan in the opening shot an arrow can be drawn to illustrate the direction of the pan. The same can be done for tracking shots and the movement of characters in the shot. Filmmakers also write down the transitions that they intend to use between shots, as guidelines for editing the footage. Many filmmakers also write down rough directions for crew and actors so that everyone knows what is going to happen in a particular shot.

Shot no.	Picture	Type of shot & duration	Sound/dialogue
13	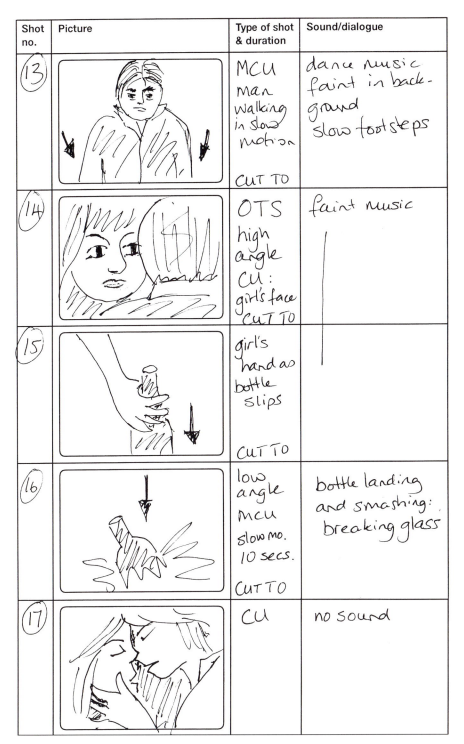	MCU man walking in slow motion CUT TO	dance music faint in back-ground slow footsteps
14		OTS high angle CU: girl's face CUT TO	faint music
15		girl's hand as bottle slips CUT TO	
16		low angle MCU slow mo. 10 secs. CUT TO	bottle landing and smashing: breaking glass
17		CU	no sound

Adapted from a storyboard provided by Sarah Mannix, student at Long Road Sixth Form College.

Though putting down this much information may seem time-consuming to students, detailed planning of the film will enable them to have a clearer idea of what they are aiming for in the finished product. It also means the filming can be more efficient as they can make shot lists for the various locations from the storyboard. Often this is important as access to the cameras can be limited.

---

student notes **Top tips for storyboarding**

- **Photocopy a set of storyboard sheets** – so you do not have to worry about continually redrawing frame outlines.
- **Draw in pencil** – to allow you to make changes easily. If you are going to photocopy the sheets remember to ink them first as pencil does not photocopy well.
- **Make short notes** – add brief directions under each frame eg

  ZOE enters from left   or

  Camera to track BEN.
- **Number the shots** – so it is easier when you are editing, and so you can bin unwanted shots.
- **Use small frames** – so that drawing the storyboard is quicker. Remember, your drawing skills are not assessed, just the clarity of your ideas.
- **Note down the camera position** – so setting up the shot is much easier and quicker.

© bfi Education 2003

Page 1 of 1   Digital Video Production

---

student notes **Camera terms**

Long shot (LS): subject is distant from the camera, surroundings dominate.

Establishing shot (ES): often a long shot, it sets the scene by establishing where the action is happening; generally used as the first shot of a sequence.

Medium shot (MS): shot where the subject and the setting are roughly in balance, so that both the person (what he/she is wearing and the expression on his/her face) and where he/she is situated is clear.

Close up (CU): the subject dominates the frame; anything from head and shoulders shot to a giant image of part of the body or part of an object, like an eye or a number on a clock face (**Extreme close up** or **ECU** can be used to describe the latter).

Pan: sideways movement of the camera from a static position (eg side to side on a tripod).

Tilt: up or down movement of the camera from a static position;

Track or dolly shot: movement of the camera on some kind of trolley, often following a character.

High angle: Shot looking down on a subject.

Low angle: Shot looking up at a subject.

Zoom: movement of the lens to go closer or move out from the subject.

© bfi Education 2003

Page 1 of 1   Digital Video Production

Storyboarding tips for students

The following tips are provided on a photocopiable handout (available at www.bfi.org.uk/tfms).

- **Use small frames** – this makes drawing the storyboard quicker and means that your drawing skills are not assessed, only the clarity of your ideas.
- **Photocopy a set of storyboard sheets** – then you do not have to worry about continually redrawing frame outlines.
- **Draw in pencil** – this allows you to make changes easily; if you are going to photocopy the sheets remember to ink them first as pencil does not photocopy well.
- **Number the shots** – this makes it easier when you are editing and helps you bin unwanted shots
- **Make short notes** – as mentioned above add some brief directions, eg ZOË enters from left, or camera to track BEN
- **Note down the camera position** – this will make setting up the shot easier and quicker.

Overall the storyboard is an important part of the filmmaking process. It is perhaps more vital to a low-budget filmmaker than to big-budget film directors, however storyboards are used by everyone (many DVDs with special features include examples of storyboards for major films). Poorly-shot student footage is often due to a lack of storyboarding and this is evident in the finished piece.

● Shooting

Camera technique

● Everyone in a group must take a turn at all parts of the work, even if some contribute more in some areas than others. As everyone did the 'driving test' all students will know how to operate the camera and the editing equipment. They must practise their skills, otherwise they will have difficulty writing about how the process worked. In any case, other group members don't want 'passengers'.

● Remind students that they must know (double check) when the record button is on and off. It is pointless to come back with two hours of shots of their walking feet and none of the material they set up!

● Likewise they must make sure date and time is not displayed on the camera viewfinder. If they are, they will be there on the final footage. Make sure students know how to switch them off.

● Auto focus can sometimes be a problem – students should know how to control manual focus.

● They should use 'Shoot!' and 'Cut!' commands and a simple **clapperboard** for easier editing later.

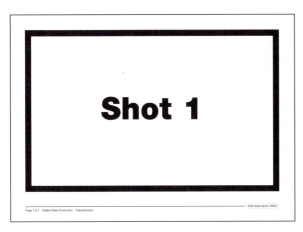

Page 1 of 1   Digital Video Production   Clapperboard   ©bfi Education 2003

This paper clapperboard consists of 16 sheets (Shot 1 – Shot 16). The sheets can be photocopied – one set for each group – and inserted in a ring binder. During shooting, the clpapperboard with the relevant shot number can be held in front of the camera at the start of each shot.

- They must keep the camera upright unless they want to turn the TV on its side to watch the footage! A well-planned tilt, however, is almost always better than a zoom, which as a rule, should be avoided since it can look amateur and make footage look like a home video. The zoom function is useful to help set up shots, but should be avoided for the actual filming.
- Students need practice at keeping the camera steady, using a tripod wherever possible. They must be sure they know how to assemble a tripod before putting a camera onto it. Hand-held footage, like point-of-view (POV) shots, is very hard to do well.

- Moving shots should be set up in advance as it is vital to know where they are going to finish before they start; students should do a test shoot, then run the camera before the opening and continue running it after the action finishes.
- Attention must be paid to framing. Shots need not always be centrally framed, but beware of close-ups where the actor moves his or her head too much, or shots where the actors' heads are right at the bottom of the frame and a big brick wall or curtain looms behind. Equally it is important that students don't just concentrate on the action in the foreground – what is happening behind? Do they want that passer-by in the background making a rude sign? Does there appear to be a tree growing out of the hero's head?

- Groups should shoot plenty of extra footage to use in editing for cutaways and cut-ins;
- They should plan reaction shots and have plenty of variety of shots (LS, MS, CU) and angles on the same subjects.

● Sound and lighting

- Students should try out built-in microphones before going out on dialogue shoots so they can decide how to compensate for their limitations. Most camera microphones pick up every sound equally (planes, the wind, distant doors slamming, as well as essential dialogue). Solutions to this problem include: shooting some scenes from behind which can be dubbed later; recording 'wild' sounds, for example, of traffic or birds singing, which can be used without the visuals with dubbed dialogue; shooting dialogue in places where there is minimal background sound; or using an external microphone (this should be tried out before being used for real).
- Students need to consider how the subject is lit. If the main source of light is behind the subject he or she will be in silhouette. In difficult light conditions, they should shoot a few frames, rewind and check. For an effective piece of cheap lighting they could take a large torch with them; but they should remember that most night shooting will produce completely dark tape – thrillers may be set at night but aren't necessarily shot at night. For mid-shots and close-ups (interior) a 60 watt bulb in a bedside lamp can be quite effective.

Content

- On an assessed project it is unwise to try to be funny. What is funny to students is unlikely to get them many marks. Humour is the most difficult form to master because it depends far more on technique than content. Students should be urged to always play it straight!
- Scenes and sequences to avoid include:
  - Endless car-based sequences which look like students showing off that they've passed their test;
  - Scenes in pubs – they look like students showing off that they can pass for 18 and get served;
  - Long scenes of kissing – these are usually just there to feature boys who want to prove they can get a girlfriend;
  - Scenes of students doing drugs (or simulating doing drugs) are painfully embarrassing;
  - Film parodies or pastiche – these have to be really good to work; every student thinks they were the first to think of doing a chocolate advert in the style of *The Blair Witch Project* (Myrick/Sanchez 1999) ... but they weren't!

● Editing

● If students have used a simple clapperboard (see page 57) in front of the camera at the start of each shot, they can do a edit on paper first which can save a lot of time in the long run.

● When editing, students should avoid cutting immediately to a second shot of the same thing; they should cut to a different subject first then cut back to the first subject – it looks more professional.

● Most transitions should be cuts; fades can be used to slow the pace. Students should be discouraged from overusing 'wacky' transitions (only good on children's TV); special effects of any kind should be kept special by limiting their use.

● Cut and cut again. Unless a shot has dialogue, the audience is likely to get the point in less than one and a half seconds, so if the shot lasts much longer, the group should ask themselves whether it couldn't be cut down. Shorter is usually better. This is particularly true in adverts. Student video shots are rarely too short, but often too long.

● In title sequences, students should not use the names of famous actors or directors – the audience will expect to see them. Check film openings to see which personnel do get a mention and stick to the relevant crew. They should use their own names or make names up, but not silly names – they should keep the tone right.

● When doing voiceovers, students must make sure that the sound level is adequate so they can be heard over the music. They should record only when the room is quiet. When choosing music, they need to avoid picking particularly popular or favourite tracks and should concentrate on finding something which suits the film.

● They must stick to the conventions of what they are producing. For example, a thriller lasts 90 minutes or more, so they don't have to tell the whole story in the first two minutes. In an opening sequence, they should aim to set up atmosphere and intrigue the viewer. Likewise an advertisement usually lasts 30 seconds or less; not only will the audience be bored by a two-minute ad but no company would be prepared to pay for such a lengthy slot!

Above all, students should treat their projects with professionalism and organisation and they will not go far wrong! Being creative is good, but you can't beat being organised.

Managing students: the role of the teacher

Apart from passing on the advice listed above, what can a teacher do to ensure the smoothest possible project work? The most important features of the teacher's job here are the same watchwords as for students: planning and organisation. You have to think ahead and plan the whole period of the project.

● Time-scale and deadlines

● Don't allow too long for the project; students have a tendency to leave things until the last minute, which is exacerbated if they can only see a long stretch ahead till the deadline. For AS practical work, we find that five weeks from first introduction of the unit through to final deadline for the writing is enough. It focuses students' minds and concentrates their efforts so that they are at their most productive. We split the year group in half so that while half the students work intensively on the practical, the other half work on an exam-based unit. At A2 we give slightly longer (two weeks of introduction, five weeks of planning, shooting and editing, two weeks of evaluation and writing) but have the whole year group working on the task simultaneously.

● Limit introductory time (at least for AS) to a few sessions in the space of a week, which should include talking through the project instructions and showing and discussing examples of previous student work.

● Keep to deadlines – unless there is a major equipment failure, don't be panicked into extending it and don't let individuals have extra time unless you have a medical note for them.

● Stagger deadlines so that you haven't got every single group trying to get on the machines with an hour to go! As long as all classes have had roughly an equal amount of time on the project, no one can complain if one class has to finish by lunch on Tuesday, another by the end of the day and another by lunch on Wednesday. It is worth counting the lessons or days available before the project starts to ensure no one is disadvantaged by the loss of time for a bank holiday or an INSET day.

● Set a limit on the amount of time each group may borrow the camera and on the number of hours of editing. You can always be a bit flexible for particularly conscientious groups later on but it helps students to know that they really will only get the camera for one weekend so they have to be organised.

● Organisation of resources and planning

● Give every group a number which students must use for booking equipment. You decide which machine they will be using and create a file for them with all the necessary materials. Label up a unique tape for them and give every group a logbook to keep details of their discussions, storyboards and attendance at sessions.

● Listen in to initial discussions and ask for small presentations either just to you or to the class as a whole regarding the intentions of the project. Be prepared to criticise ideas which you know to be unworkable or over-ambitious; in the end it is better to force a rethink at an early stage than to let students loose on something which is doomed to failure.

● Insist that no group may use the camera without showing you prior evidence of planning, especially storyboards. When students return from shooting and import their footage, set a limit as to how much footage they may keep in their folder on the computer. By the end of the session they must either have deleted any excess footage or you will delete it for them as others need to use the machine too.

● Monitoring who does what – get involved

● Keep a check on editing by asking to see what the groups have done so far at least once a session. Be prepared to intervene by asking what a sequence is supposed to mean if it seems unclear, or by criticising material which does not work. You will not be doing their project for them but constructively supporting their work. Be prepared to comment on titles, choice of music, editing, transitions and effects as well as the raw footage itself. If it really should be improved and there is an opportunity to do so, then make them shoot it again!

Facilitating effective evaluation

● When you remove the edited projects, get them onto a viewable format as swiftly as possible so that you can have follow-up sessions when you screen and discuss the students' work. These sessions are crucial to the evaluation process as both you and the rest of the class can give each group feedback. They need tight structuring and a summary of points noted on the board may be useful. Insist students take notes to help when they write up the project.

● Though students should be encouraged to write their evaluations as they work on the project, it is inevitable that most will leave it until the end. Though they need time to reflect on the finished video and to take feedback, they do not need ages to work on the writing. Even a 2000 word write-up can be completed inside a week. It may be useful to provide some notes for structuring these essays, and those who want help with drafts can be encouraged to come and show you. Those who leave it until the last minute, always will ...

● Celebrate student work – special screening events

Try to organise a special screening of all the projects to create a sense of occasion and celebration of the work. If you are able to book a local cinema screen for the morning and they have video projection facilities, this can be a real motivator, both for meeting deadlines and ensuring a high quality of finished product. Students can invite parents or friends along (especially those who have appeared in the videos). It also provides an opportunity to invite senior management to see what you have done with the money you were allocated. You might even get a reporter from the local paper to come and cover the event.

● Show-reels

The projects themselves should be seen as much more than just an exercise to be marked and moderated; apart from the special event screening, individual student show-reels can be made to aid students' entry into university. Show-reels can also be made to:

- Show to future students to help them learn from past successes and failures; this may help to improve still further the Centre's standard of work;
- Show at events like open evenings;
- Remind management what students have achieved in your department.

We would argue that the single biggest attraction for prospective students at our college open evenings has been the videos on show and the possibility of doing such work themselves.

Planning – schemes of work

Finally, plan your scheme of work so that the students get two attempts at the production unit. (See the sample schemes of work on pp11–19.) By placing this at the centre of your course, you will increase motivation levels and raise performance substantially. Our students undertake one practical in the Autumn term, learn from it and then do another in the Spring term. On the whole the one in the Spring term is better as a result of the steep learning curve they have undergone. Students take both practicals seriously, but by the second they have acquired sufficient skills to make the most of their understanding and the equipment. The same is true of their writing, which improves a lot by producing two evaluations which follow a defined format but deal with different material.

As suggested in the report on the BECTA project:

> '... recursive opportunities for DV work would have a significant impact on the quality of work produced. Much work with DV in the past has been characterised as 'one-off' opportunities, where pupils never have the chance to revisit pieces of work or try out new techniques, and where the emphasis has been less on learning than on celebrating the fact that anything has been produced at all.' (p8)

Evaluation and assessment

● Making evaluation meaningful

There has long been a real danger in Media Studies that the written evaluation (or log or commentary, or whatever else it may be called in a particular specification) is seen as more important than the production work itself. This danger is compounded if there are expectations of a complex theoretical account, which bears little relation to the project undertaken. At its best, the written evaluation should be a truly reflective piece of writing, which looks closely at the production process and the finished project and attempts to engage with what has actually been learnt from the process. However, such writing can be better achieved if teachers provide a template (see below).

The following points are worth keeping in mind:

- Any evaluative writing should be word-processed. This makes it easier for you to help by looking at drafts and suggesting improvements as the work progresses.
- Students should be encouraged to keep their writing clear, simple and systematic, following the suggested template you provide.
- They should be discouraged from filling their writing with excuses. They need to be honest about the shortcomings of their own work and make it clear what they have learnt from the experience, without blaming things on other members of the group, limited equipment or worst of all, their teachers!
- They must keep within the word limit, as this is part of the assessment and they risk a penalty if they fail to do so.
- Their writing will probably need to address all the Key Concepts of audience, institution, forms and conventions, and representations (variations on the wording of key concepts exist with different specifications, but are essentially concerned with the same important ideas). The best way to do this is to focus upon the text produced and its context.

Here are some key generic questions, which an effective evaluation should address (**Worksheet 6**):

- Who is it aimed at? How would such an audience be targeted? How did the audience which viewed the piece actually respond? Students could pose some open questions to the audience at the screening about the video and the meanings which it generates, the responses to which they can include in their evaluation.

- Where would such a product appear in the media? What kind of institution would play it or produce it? What similar products are there and how are these placed and sold?

- How is the product constructed and what conventions does it use? How do these compare with real media examples of similar products? You should draw comparisons wherever possible.

- What social groups does the video represent? How far are these representations typical and how far not? In what ways can the representations be compared with similar kinds of text from real media?

Assessing work

The end of the project is the assessment of work which will subsequently be sent for moderation. The assessment must be carried out properly if the project is to get the credit it deserves. Assessment of finished products has to make close reference to the criteria set by the relevant awarding body's specification.

It is useful to start the process of assessment as early as possible. In each of the different specifications, there is some element of credit awarded for the planning process. You can start to observe and make some written notes on this from the outset, and use them in the final marking process. Individual contributions to the group product, and their understanding of the technology and techniques used, will need to be assessed and this cannot simply be 'read off' a finished product. The nature of video-making (particularly shooting) is such that you cannot hope to have observed everything but where observation is possible it is always useful to make notes which will make the final assessment that much easier.

All criteria are open to interpretation and one person's 'Competent' may well be another's 'Proficient'. However, it is possible to be consistent in assessing a cohort's work, particularly if they are working on a common task. The bottom line with all practical work must be an understanding of how to use the medium to make meaning; this, in turn, is manifested in adherence to conventions and technical ability with the equipment. If you and your students follow the guidelines above you should achieve a good standard of work every time.

Finally, though acquisition of digital equipment will not guarantee all your students Grade 'A's, it makes the tools available so they can learn more quickly and demonstrate their understanding more completely in fully-realised productions.

Managing bigger projects: making a music video

In this section we will look at the process of producing a music video. Overall a project such as this requires a lot of planning. You need to be familiar with the editing program that the students will use, as music videos can be fairly 'effects-heavy'. You also need to be clear about how you will structure this type of activity. It is easier to complete this type of project in a set time scale – five weeks is enough for a video to be planned, shot and edited successfully.

You can use this project outside a formal educational setting as it has the potential to engage young people in a variety of contexts. Outside a coursework context, it would be possible for students to choose their own music, but this needs to be managed so that the planning, filming and editing still takes priority over the choice of music. It could also be adapted to fit in with an induction programme where students have to make a video from footage that has been collected or shot by staff and then edit it to a set audio track. Overall it is an exercise that is both enjoyable and rewarding which, after all, is what a project should be! With careful planning and good organisation students can produce high quality work.

The management of this project includes:

- providing the students with the theoretical knowledge that they need;
- the technical elements of music videos;
- the management of student groups;
- the physical production of the video;
- presentation to an audience and feedback;
- written evaluation;
- teacher assessment.

● The Task

The task for this project is to take material by an unknown band (for reasons explained later) and produce a music promo for the release of a single.

● Preparation

This starts with some introductory work on the music industry, which particularly focuses on music videos. It is important to show a wide range of music videos covering different genres, identifying the stylistic elements that make certain genres unique. A distinctive genre, for example, is experimental electronic music, such as in Chris Cunningham's videos (for bands/artists such as Aphex Twins). Most students are likely to spend more time than most teachers watching music videos, so it is worth getting hold of current videos or there will be confusion over what constitutes a music video. It is also useful to show previous student work as this generally provokes the most comments and is often nearer the standard that the students will produce.

It is useful to provide students with a framework for analysing music video which can be applied to both professional and student work. Andrew Goodwin, in his book on the rise of MTV, *Dancing in the Distraction Factory* (1992), identifies a number of key features which distinguish the music video as a form:

- There is a relationship between the lyrics and the visuals (with visuals either illustrating, amplifying or contradicting the lyrics).
- There is a relationship between the music and the visuals (again with visuals either illustrating, amplifying or contradicting the music).
- Particular music genres may have their own music video style and iconography (such as live stage performance in heavy rock).
- There will be a demand on the part of the record company for lots of close-ups of the main artist or vocalist.
- There is likely to be reference to voyeurism, particularly in the treatment of females, but also in terms of systems of looking (screens within screens, binoculars, cameras, etc).
- There are likely to be intertextual references, either to other music videos or to films and TV texts.

This framework can be applied to any music video, including the students' own production.

● Pre-production

The music

Rather than allow students to choose their own music, you should offer them unfamiliar material from a range of genres, sourced primarily from the internet where MP3 sites offer a large number of unsigned bands. You could also use material from the darker corners of your (and your colleagues) record collections (though you risk students either ridiculing the choice or ruining a favourite album through their visual interpretation!). Collect the material in sets of three tracks, renaming the bands to prevent students being influenced by an existing band image.

Pre-selected music has several advantages:

● It is easier for students to construct an original image for a band they have not heard of.
● There is less likelihood of students 'borrowing' footage from a chosen band's video and claiming it is their own (remember their knowledge of music videos is likely to be greater than yours).
● It provides the students with a broader selection than they would otherwise choose.
● It lowers the chance of students using the same material.
● It allows students to take a more professional approach to the material as they are in the same position as real music video directors, who do not have to *like* the material in order to do a good job.

The pitch

Once you have completed the introduction to the task, the students can start the planning process, which includes the selection of the artist/group on which they wish to work. In choosing a track, they should think in terms of generating visual ideas rather than simply illustrating the lyrics.

Before commencing work with their chosen music, students are asked to make a 'pitch' for the particular artist they have chosen and provided no more than two groups pick the same band, they will get their choice. If however, three or more groups opt for one choice, you have to decide on the best two and the other groups must start again. This degree of early pressure helps focus students' initial planning. It is an opportunity to discuss how and why the group intends to do things and to prevent any over-ambitious projects from being started. The pitch also offers students the chance to ask for advice on how to achieve particular effects and to be advised on the limitations of the edit program. If a group is unsuccessful in pitching for their chosen music they have to select again and re-pitch. They must come up with new ideas here, otherwise it somewhat defeats the object of the process.

The groups then have five weeks to plan, shoot and edit the music video.

Storyboarding

Once the 'pitch' has been approved the groups start to storyboard the video. This is an important process that allows the students to clarify their initial ideas on paper. Storyboarding is a good exercise as it helps groups think about locations and props that they will need. The storyboard for a music video is both an essential starting point and editing tool. Students must use a variety of camera angles and shot distances, which should be shown in the storyboard.

With music videos it is important to remember that there is no need to tell a story or for complex narrative ideas. Often such ideas dilute the quality of the video as a promotional tool, as students will focus on the story and not on producing a simple yet effective music video.

● Production – shooting

The guidelines on pp57–8 may be useful here.

- Students should check that all the equipment is working, that they have everything that they need, and that the right tape is loaded.
- Each group is only allowed to borrow a camera kit once they have shown you their storyboard and discussed it with you. This helps focus the group's work and gives you an idea of how the project is progressing. You could ask questions at this stage about where and how the group intends to shoot the video.
- Camera equipment can be borrowed over a weekend or for two overnight shoots. Groups can also use the camera during lessons. As long as groups know that camera use is limited they tend to be focused while filming and very productive.
- When shooting a performance-based video it is worth taking a CD player on location, to play the chosen track.
- It is a good idea to shoot the performance three or more times from a number of different angles as this will give groups a lot of footage to use when editing and prevent the performance from becoming boring.
- When shooting the video the students should use their storyboards and shot lists and shoot more footage than they think they will need as this will make the editing easier.
- Students should try to avoid just illustrating the lyrics.
- They can use cutaway shots. You could demonstrate this technique by getting students to study professional examples. It will also make the editing easier and give the video a more professional finish.

● Editing

Once the students have finished shooting, the raw footage is imported onto the computer where students are encouraged to begin the process of cutting it down. The audio track that the students have chosen is imported into the editing program that they are using and saved in their folder.

Given the amount that groups shoot and the size of the hard drives, it is important that the first session of editing involves removing footage that will never be used, including takes that have not been successful. This serves a dual purpose: it frees space on the computer hard drive and it helps to focus the students on keeping the project manageable. In some cases it will also reveal that a group has not shot enough material and needs to film more to make a successful video.

Students can use two different editing packages, either iMovie or Adobe Premiere (see pp 41–5 for comparisons); however, all students should import their footage into iMovie initially, and those intending to use Première should then export batches into QuickTime before final importing them into Première. This speeds up the process of deleting unwanted material. Even iMovie projects could go through Premiere when they are finished as processing in Première allows compression of the soundtrack which makes the audio sound better during playback on VCRs and on cinema sound systems.

Good footage can be made into an effective video if it is tightly edited. Students find it difficult to sustain tight editing beyond three minutes, so the track they select should be between two and a half and three minutes long. This will help them make the most of their footage and generally enable them to produce better edited videos. They may need to cut down the music beforehand – easily done in a sound edit program or in Première.

Students should use their storyboard while editing the video as this will provide the starting point. Once they are underway they are likely to deviate from this, perhaps preferring alternative set-ups that they shot. This is no problem provided they have planned the basics!

Editing is the point at which effects can be added; with this in mind it is important that students are aware of the technical limitations of the program. They must also continually save their work; students often forget to save work before they render it, something every machine will need to do. By saving their work continually they should prevent any major problems.

Editing is likely to be the stage that most groups spend longest on and they should allocate at least two weeks to it, so that all the required effects can be added, as well as to avoid a rush when it comes to processing the finished projects. Around eight to ten hours of editing time will probably be needed and more complex projects, involving animations or other effects, may take much longer.

Students working in Première, who have been through several projects in iMovie, tend not to rely on the multitude of effects available but to use just cuts, fades and dissolves plus one or two largely 'invisible' tricks such as motion effects. This indicates a maturity in their work as they are not trying to disguise poor or unplanned footage through effects.

● Evaluation

As suggested on p 63, the finished videos could be showcased at a local cinema. This event has great status and justifies the tight deadline you have given students, since if any group were not to finish on time, their work would not be shown. Seeing their videos projected on a thirty-foot screen means every blemish will be noticeable, so there is intensified incentive to produce high quality work. Subsequent screening in class time gives a second opportunity for others to see the work and this time to give more intimate feedback. You should also give feedback individually to each group to assist their evaluation essays which are an important part of the finished product.

Student's essays

Once students have completed the production of the music video they must write a critical evaluation or commentary on their work. They will need a template to help them write effective and focused evaluations (**Worksheet 7**).

The evaluation should cover all stages of production, if necessary referring to any problems encountered in the production stages, but students should avoid blaming others for the shortcomings of the product. It should cover all technical aspects, including techniques used to give the video a certain look. It is in the best interests of students to be honest and carefully explain what has been done, remembering that using editing software creatively is as important as having interesting ideas. They should also explain what their individual inputs to the project were. This allows students the opportunity to explain what they have done, especially if their influence has been more subtle than that of more vocal members of their group.

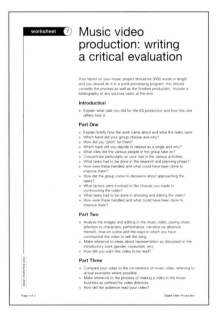

Students will also need to provide an analysis of their own videos which may require the application of a theoretical framework; Andrew Goodwin's framework is particularly suitable for music videos. In this part of the evaluation, students should expand on why decisions were made and what they hoped their effects would achieve. They should discuss why the video has a narrative or why not, and whether this fits with the genre of music represented. It is also worth discussing why individuals or social groups are represented in a particular way. Again this may link to a specific genre of music.

This is also the opportunity for students to discuss intertextuality, which may mean mentioning influences on the narrative structure or other texts that have been referred to. As before they should be as honest as possible, by crediting intertextual references. It shows an understanding of wider texts to be upfront about where their ideas have come from rather than trying to pass off 'borrowed' ideas or footage as their own. While students should make reference to existing texts and products in relation to their own to demonstrate their research process, these should be relevant to their own production. Specific references should be made to other music videos or texts to illustrate how their video relates to the genre or how it alters generic conventions. The more examples of other videos that they can use the stronger their arguments can be.

The evaluation is also an opportunity to include feedback from an audience. This should go beyond a sentence claiming the video to be successfu. It should allow students to critique their own work based on the comments of others. Have their concepts been understood? Did the audience interpret the video as they intended or did it cause confusion? Though the video may be an original concept it could suffer from poor editing or camerawork, so how does this affect the audience's understanding?

Assessing the work

It is vital that assessment is focused upon the criteria from the specification you are working from. Common problems in the assessment of music video work stem from the teacher's lack of knowledge of the form itself and particularly of individual musical genres within it. It is tempting to be over-generous with marks for something with which you are unfamiliar. However, as a guiding principle, we would suggest always taking account of the following:

● How well has this group worked on research and planning?
● How well have they applied general principles of camerawork, editing and use of *mise en scène*?
● Can they use the equipment properly?
● Can we separate out the contribution of different individuals? All specifications take some account of this and we should expect in some groups that the marks will reflect very different levels of participation, although in many 'good' groups the marks may not differ that much if all have worked well.

- How much does this 'look' like a music video? Is it enough to say 'It's got music and it's a video, therefore it's a music video'?
- If the music is from an unfamiliar genre (to you), ask to see some of the examples which they quote from real videos as providing their 'models.
- In your comments to support your marks on students' work/assessment cover sheets, try to be as clear as possible on how you have used the criteria and how you have arrived at your marks. It is much harder for a moderator to argue with well-supported marks.

A final word on creativity

Our view of creativity echoes that of the authors of the BECTA report (2002). We do not equate creativity with originality and freedom from constraint; far from being hands off, the teacher has an important role in supporting pupils' creative processes.

> 'The authors of this report would argue … that originality is a necessary but not sufficient, precondition for creative work, and that teachers setting and pupils understanding clear constraints for creative tasks is likely to generate the best work from pupils.' (p25)

We believe, like them, that there must be a 'clear relationship in the work produced between creativity and moving image literacy' and find their definition of creative work in Media Studies quite a useful one

> '… a kind of creative apprenticeship, where some degree of imitation of conventional forms such as trailers, pop videos and television dramas is a necessary point of departure, from which more sophisticated creative work such as pastiche, parody and subversion of generic conventions can follow.' (p89)

Conclusion

Digital video has transformed our experience as teachers over the past three years and opened up opportunities for our students which are envied by previous generations. Placing it at the centre of our curriculum has produced a greater degree of enthusiasm and motivation than we have ever enjoyed previously. It has also affected social learning most positively and, in turn, fed into theoretical understanding of what might be termed broader media literacy in a powerful way. It has not been cheap and it has taken a lot of organisation, but it has certainly made the media classroom a 21st century environment of collaborative learning.

Glossary

Analogue
The way in which video was shot and edited before digital video was developed.

Auto focus
The feature on a camera which automatically focus on what is in the centre of the viewfinder/lens.

AVID
A professional, industry standard digital editing system, used by many filmmakers.

Bin
A term used in some edit programs to describe the folder in which clips are stored.

Capture
The act of moving footage from camera to computer.

Capture card (sound/video)
An additional piece of hardware needed on the computer in order to take in footage from an external source such as a camera.

CD-ROM
A compact disc on which data is stored.

Chromakey
A feature which allows subjects to be filmed against a plain (blue or green) background which, at the editing stage, can be replaced with a pictorial background (eg to show a character apparently flying through the sky).

Clapperboard
A numbered sign, which is held in front of the camera before each shot is filmed, allowing the reconstruction of the footage during editing in a completely different order to be accomplished more easily.

Clips
Individual shots or short sequences.

Dedicated
Used only for one purpose.

Digital
A process which uses 0s and 1s to describe data which, for our purposes, means the material coded is of higher quality and more flexible than analogue material.

Distribution
The means of getting media texts to their audience.

Download
Putting data onto a computer hard drive.

Drag/Drop
Using the mouse pointer to move a clip from the shelf or bin to the timeline.

DVD (Digital Versatile Disk)
A disk storing large amounts of data (4.7GB) such as a film.

Evaluation
Here, this refers to the writing about practical work which students are required to do.

Export
The process of taking edited material off the computer onto video or CD or DVD.

Film (noun, as in celluloid)
The raw material used by filmmakers in traditional cinema.

FireWire
The link used to import footage onto or export from a computer, via a lead which allows different types of hardware to 'communicate' at high speed.

Gigabyte (GB)
1000 million bytes of data, the equivalent of about 700 floppy disks or two CDs.

Hard drive (integral/external)
The storage device on a computer, usually of 20GB or more in capacity. External hard drives allow storage of more material and enable it to be moved from one computer to another.

Hardware
Computers, cameras and other technology which form the base for video work.

i-Link
A particular form of FireWire connection developed by Sony.

Import
Similar to capture, the means of getting footage onto the computer.

Interface
The connection between pieces of hardware.

LCD
Liquid Crystal Display, used in monitors on computers and also the mini-screens on video cameras.

Linear editing
The traditional method of editing, constructing the film by editing footage in the same sequence as the finished running order of shots.

Manual focus
An option available on most cameras to override the auto focus, so the camera operator can choose which element should be sharp in the frame.

Megabyte (MB)
One million bytes of information – about equivalent to the amount that can fit on a floppy disk.

Non-linear editing
The way in which digital editing works – the user can edit in any order and re-edit an infinite number of times.

Package
A computer program.

Peripherals
The extra bits of equipment which might be added to the basic set-up.

Platform
A computer system such as Mac or PC.

Port
A socket used to connect a peripheral device to a computer, such as a printer or a camera.

Post-production
The stage after shooting and editing.

Pre-production
The planning stages, before shooting starts.

Production
The main shooting and editing stages.

RAM
The 'memory' of the computer needed to run programs.

Rendering
The process used by image and video programs to activate the effects or other processes requested by the user (such as adding a title or transition).

RGB cable
A standard video cable to connect VCR to TV

S-video
A system which gives higher quality than VHS and can be used to connect some VCRs to TVs.

Set-ups (camera)
Different positions used for each shot.

Shelf
Similar to the bin in some programs, a storage area on screen for clips.

Software
The program or raw materials needed for a project, such as CD or video tape.

Storyboard
A planning sheet on which shots can be drawn prior to shooting.

Take
A version of the shot. If several versions are taken, the best 'take' might be chosen for the final film.

Timeline
On the screen, as part of the edit program, the basic work area where clips in use are stored.

Transitions
Fades, dissolves, wipes etc which overlap between shots to move the video from one shot to another.

Zip drive
A device which allows the transfer of data from one computer to another, with a ZIP disk, usually 100MB maximum in size.

References and bibliography

J Bennett, T Jones, J McDougall and R Harvey (2002) *A2 Media Studies for OCR*, Hodder

D Bordwell and K Thompson (2001) *Film Art: An Introduction*, 6th ed, McGraw-Hill

D Buckingham, J Grahame and J Sefton-Green (1995) *Making Media – Practical Production in Media Education*, English and Media Centre

A Burn and J Durran (1998) 'Going Non-linear', *Trac 2*

V Clark, J Baker and E Lewis (2002) *Key Concepts and Skills for Media Studies*, Hodder

S Donaldson, T Thornicroft and M Reid (2001), *An Introduction to Film Language*, CD-ROM, bfi

E Elsey and A Kelly (2002) *In Short: A Guide to Short Film-making in the Digital Age*, bfi

B Ferguson (1981) 'Practical Work and Pedagogy', *Screen Education*, no 38

A Goodwin (1992), *Dancing in the Distraction Factory*, Routledge

C Jones and G Jolliffe (1996) *The Guerilla Film Maker's Handbook*, Cassell

T Jones, J McDougall, J Bennett, J Bowker and R Harvey (2001) *AS Media Studies for OCR*, Hodder

L Masterman (1980) *Teaching about Television*, Macmillan

M Readman (2003): *Teaching Scriptwriting, Screenplays and Storyboards for Film and TV Production*, Teaching Film and Media Studies series, bfi

M Reid, A Burn and D Parker (2002), *Evaluation of the BECTA Digital Video Project*, BECTA. Available to download in PDF format from: http://www.becta.org.uk/research/reports/digitalvideo/index.cfm

Picture Power CD-ROM The English and Media Centre www.englishandmedia.co.uk

W P Robertson and T Cooke (1998), *The Big Lebowski – The Making of a Coen Brothers' Film*, Faber

E Scarratt (2003): *Teaching Analysis of Film Language and Production*, Teaching Film and Media Studies series, bfi

R Stafford and G Branston (1999) *The Media Studies Students' Book*, Routledge

C Stewart, M Lavelle and A Kowlatzke (2001) *Media and Meaning: An Introduction*, bfi

R Thompson (1997) *The Grammar of the Edit*, Focal Press

Software manuals

D Pogue (2000) *iMovie2: The Missing Manual*, Pogue Press/O'Reilly

There is a plethora of manuals, under several titles, for example, *For Dummies*, *For Idiots*, *Classroom in a Book* etc. They can be found by searching for the software program name in online bookstores, such as Amazon. www.amazon.co.uk

Websites

National awarding bodies

AQA – GCSE, AS/A level, GNVQ, AVCE Media Studies
www.aqa.org.uk/qual/gceasa/med.html

EdExcel – GNVQ, AVCE Media Studies
www.edexcel.org.uk

OCR – GCSE, AS/A level, GNVQ, AVCE Media Studies
www.ocr.org.uk/develop/media_st/mediastd.htm – specifications
   Visit the experimental support site at
   http://ital-dev.ucles-red.cam.ac.uk/listsupport/ocr-mediastudies-a
   for teaching resources, FAQs, etc
Mediastudies-a@community.ocr.org.uk
A free online professional community, run by email, for media teachers
   following OCR specifications. The archived messages have significant
   information and advice from teachers and examiners on digital video
   editing.

SQA – Higher and Advanced Higher Media Studies
www.sqa.org.uk

WJEC – GCSE, AS/A level Media Studies, AS/A level Film Studies
www.wjec.co.uk

Suppliers

Adobe   www.adobe.co.uk

Apple   www.apple.com

Jessops   www.jessops.co.uk

Microsoft   www.microsoft.com/uk

Solutions   www.solutions-inc.co.uk/education and
www.solutions-inc.co.uk/sections/dv.html
An Apple Education dealer, with comprehensive digital video editing and
camera product information, free online resources, educational research
projects and a regular email newsletter, based in Brighton, Sussex (but
who can put schools/colleges in touch with Apple Education dealers in
their area if necessary). Also for information on Pinnacle and Matrox
products.

Sony   www.sony.co.uk

Top Tape of Harrow   http://web.ukonline.co.uk/rollon/note.htm

Sources of downloadable **music** for use with student music videos,
especially by unknown bands:
www.mp3.com
www.peoplesound.co.uk
www.icrunch.co.uk

Shooting People   http://.shootingpeople.org
A service for filmmakers and TV production personnel, with an email alert
subscription service with details of jobs and projects, which might be
useful for students seeking work experience.

Skillset   www.skillset.org
Information from the main media industry training organisation.

Educational Contacts

In addition to the teaching resources, national conferences, MA modules and
INSET/student study events provided by the British Film Institute
(www.bfi.org.uk), the following organisations are of useful support to teachers:

BECTA   www.becta.org.uk

Creativity in Digital Video Awards – *Teaching and learning using digital
video*
A free CD-ROM was produced in Autumn 2002. The CD-ROM contains case
studies of the films made by pupils. It also contains both a Technical and a
Film Language glossary. It is also illustrated with stills of pupils working taken
from the digital video pilot. It contains information about using digital video in
teaching and learning and includes ideas on how to get started, choosing
technology and software, plus hints, tips, FAQs and other advice and
resources. The CD-ROM also contains the findings from BECTA's digital

video pilot, and films of pupils using this technology and examples of their work. You can request a copy by sending an email to dvcdrom@becta.org.uk – remember to include your postal address.

DV in Education   www.dvineducation.org.uk
A collaboration between Film Education and Denbighshire ICT Centre, which offers training courses.

The English and Media Centre   www.englishandmedia.co.uk
18 Compton Terrace, Islington, London N1 2UN
Tel: 020 7359 8080
A source of teaching resources and teacher INSET, including a magazine especially for students, *MMagazine*, which features writing from A level students, examiners and teachers on a wide range of topics. The Winter 2002 edition included a free CD-Rom of student media production from Long Road Sixth Form College.

Film Education   www.filmeducation.org
Alhambra House, 27– 31 Charing Cross Road, London WC2H 0AV. Tel: 020 7976 2297
Teaching resources, an annual film festival for schools/colleges and INSET courses.

in the picture   www.itpmag.demon.co.uk
in the picture, 36 Hospital Road, Riddlesden, Keighley BD20 5EU. Tel: 01535 663737
A termly magazine, edited by Roy Stafford, which features articles on all aspects of media education, including student production, and which also produces teaching resources and an INSET programme.

Keynote Educational Ltd   www.keynote.org.uk
PO Box 130, Wilmslow, SK9 6FN. Tel: 01625 532974
A provider of a range of national INSET training courses for Film/Media Studies teachers, including media production guidance.

Media Ed   www.MediaEd.org.uk
A website devoted to media education, which includes a teachers' forum, events diary and free resources, including a section on digital video editing by Tom Barrance, Director of Media Education Wales.
www.MediaEd.org.uk/dv.html – digital video entry page

Philip Allan Updates   www.philipallan.co.uk
A provider of national teacher INSET, student conferences and publications for Film and Media Studies teachers.

Acknowledgements

We are grateful for the assistance of our colleagues Steve Thorne and Tom Woodcock for advice on elements of this book.

PITTSBURGH FILMMAKERS
477 MELWOOD AVENUE
PITTSBURGH, PA 15213